University of Washington Alumnae Board

Profits from this cookbook and our annual Holiday Fair enable the University of Washington Alumnae Board to award 25 to 30 full-tuition scholarships to UW students each year.

Thank you for your support.

About this cookbook...

Forty-eight restaurants and chefs
throughout the state of Washington
generously submitted delicious recipes
as well as logos and photos.

★

They graciously answered our cooking questions
and provided us with interesting information.

★

Their efforts will translate into scholarships
for deserving UW students.

★

*We wish to thank each and every one of them
for the time they invested in this project.*

Alphabetical Listing of Restaurants

Restaurant	Recipe	Page
12th Avenue Cafe	Dragon Soup	33
Alligator Pear	Roasted Tomato Soup	35
Assaggio	Cappelletti alla Mauro	79
Barking Frog	Seared Ahi Tuna with Potato Rosti with Soy Emulsion and Chives	81
C Shop, The	Carmel Apples	125
Cactus!	Conchita Pibil	85
Calcutta Grill, The	Goat Cheese Scallion Spoon Bread	37
Canlis	Canlis Salad	39
Captain Whidbey Inn, The	Captain Whidbey's Penn Cove Ginger Mussels	89
	Tomato Basil Vinaigrette	45
Chateau Ste. Michelle	Argentinean Style Mixed Grill	91

Alphabetical Listing of Restaurants *continued*

Restaurant	Recipe	Page
Chuckanut Manor	Broccoli Salad	47
	Chuckanut Manor Crab Au Gratin	95
Coho Cafe	Applewood Smoked Salmon	97
Columbia Tower Club	Sauté of Wild Mushrooms and Whipped Brie on Crostini	1
Dahlia Lounge	White Chocolate Bread Pudding	127
Daniel's Broiler	Filet Strips Teriyaki	3
Earth & Ocean	Warm, Truffled Asparagus with Aged Gouda and Endive	49
Famous Northwest Catering Company, The	Vanilla Bean Cheesecake with Fresh Fruit Topping	131
Fleming's Prime Steakhouse & Wine Bar	Barbecue Cajun Shrimp	51
Gilbert's on Main	Apple Walnut Gorgonzola Salad	53

Restaurant	Recipe	Page
Herbfarm, The	Lemon Verbena-Yogurt Panna Cotta	135
Hunt Club (Sorrento Hotel)	Alaskan Halibut with Tagliatelle of Vegetables, Beurre Blanc and American Caviar	99
Il Terrazo Carmine	Calamari in Padella	5
Juanita Bay Sports Pub and Eatery	Peasant Sausage Soup	57
Kingfish Cafe, The	Macaroni and Cheese	103
Le Pichet, Restaurant	Gratin Lyonnais (Lyon-Style Onion Soup)	59
Lowell-Hunt Catering	Wild Mushroom Soup	61
Macrina Bakery & Cafe	Cherry Almond Scones	137
Maltby Cafe, The	Maltby Cafe Marionberry Pie	141
'O hana	Ahi Nori Tempura	7
Palace Kitchen, The	Goat Cheese Fondue	9
Paradiso, Ristorante	Cannelloni di Fabrizio	105

Alphabetical Listing of Restaurants *continued*

Restaurant	Recipe	Page
Pasta & Co.	Chicken Baked in Pasta & Co. Roasted Tomato Chutney Sauce	111
Ray's Boathouse	Ray's Boathouse Thai Mussels	11
Restaurant Le Pichet	Gratin Lyonnais (Lyon-Style Onion Soup)	59
Restaurant Zoë	Grilled Romaine Salad with Apples, Smoked Bacon and Roquefort Dressing	73
Ristorante Paradiso	Cannelloni di Fabrizio	105
Rover's Restaurant	Warm Alaskan Halibut Salad with Tomato Marinade	65
Roy's Seattle	Northwest Salmon Satay with Maui Onion Dipping Sauce	13
Salish Lodge & Spa	Beignets and Chocolate Coffee Ice Cream	143
	Mint and Nut Crusted Rack of Lamb with Russian Banana Fingerling Potato Purée	113

Restaurant	Recipe	Page
Saluté of Bellevue	Italian Meatballs	117
San Carlos Restaurant	San Carlos Salsa	17
Savory Faire	Amaretto Bread Pudding	149
Seastar Restaurant & Raw Bar	Halibut Ceviche with Pico de Gallo Relish	21
Semiahmoo Resort	Roasted Beets with Whole Grain Mustard, Orange and Sheep's Milk Cheese	67
SkyCity at the Needle *(Space Needle)*	Alderwood Smoked Salmon with Sushi Rice Cakes	119
	SkyCity Crab Cakes with Curry Aïoli and Apple Salsa	23
Sostanza	Stuffed Pork Loin	121
Space Needle *(SkyCity at the Needle)*	Alderwood Smoked Salmon with Sushi Rice Cakes	119
	SkyCity Crab Cakes with Curry Aïoli and Apple Salsa	23

Restaurant	Recipe	Page
Sunflour Bakery & Cafe	Grand Marnier-Chocolate Cheesecake	151
Sweet Addition	Asparagus, Prosciutto & Basil Aïoli on Baguette	27
Szmania's Restaurant	Lobster Mashed Potatoes	69
Tosoni's Restaurant	Portabello Mushroom Appetizer	29
Zoë, Restaurant	Grilled Romaine Salad with Apples, Smoked Bacon and Roquefort Dressing	73

Please Note:
The recipes in this book were submitted with the understanding
that they would be for personal use only.
Many of the recipes are copyrighted.
Commercial use is prohibited.

Table of Contents

Introduction   Page

Welcome i

About this Cookbook ii

Alphabetical Listing of Restaurants iii

Appetizers   Recipe

Columbia Tower Club .... Sauté of Wild Mushrooms and
                              Whipped Brie on Crostini. 1

Daniel's Broiler .... Filet Strips Teriyaki 3

Il Terrazo Carmine .... Calamari in Padella 5

'O hana .... Ahi Nori Tempura 7

Palace Kitchen, The .... Goat Cheese Fondue 9

Ray's Boathouse .... Ray's Boathouse Thai Mussels 11

Table of Contents *continued*

Appetizers *continued*	**Recipe**	**Page**
Roy's Seattle	Northwest Salmon Satay with Maui Onion Dipping Sauce	13
San Carlos Restaurant	San Carlos Salsa	17
Seastar Restaurant &Raw Bar	Halibut Ceviche with Pico de Gallo Relish	21
SkyCity at the Needle *(Space Needle)*	SkyCity Crab Cakes with Curry Aïoli and Apple Salsa	23
Sweet Addition	Asparagus, Prosciutto & Basil Aïoli on Baguette	27
Tosoni's Restaurant	Portabello Mushroom Appetizer	29

Soups, Salads & Sides

12th Avenue Cafe	Dragon Soup	33
Alligator Pear	Roasted Tomato Soup	35
Calcutta Grill, The	Goat Cheese Scallion Spoon Bread	37

Soups, Salads & Sides *continued*   Page

Canlis	Canlis Salad	39
Captain Whidbey Inn, The	Tomato Basil Vinaigrette	45
Chuckanut Manor	Broccoli Salad	47
Earth & Ocean	Warm, Truffled Asparagus with Aged Gouda and Endive	49
Fleming's Prime Steakhouse & Wine Bar	Barbecue Cajun Shrimp	51
Gilbert's on Main	Apple Walnut Gorgonzola Salad	53
Juanita Bay Sports Pub and Eatery	Peasant Sausage Soup	57
Le Pichet, Restaurant	Gratin Lyonnais (Lyon-Style Onion Soup)	59
Lowell-Hunt Catering	Wild Mushroom Soup	61
Rover's Restaurant	Warm Alaskan Halibut Salad with Tomato Marinade	65

Table of Contents

Table of Contents *continued*

Soups, Salads & Sides *continued*   **Page**

Semiahmoo Resort . . . . Roasted Beets with Whole Grain Mustard,
                                  Orange and Sheep's Milk Cheese 67

Szmania's Restaurant . . . . Lobster Mashed Potatoes 69

Zoë, Restaurant . . . . Grilled Romaine Salad with Apples,
                                  Smoked Bacon and Roquefort Dressing 73

Entrées

Assaggio . . . . Cappelletti alla Mauro 79

Barking Frog . . . . Seared Ahi Tuna with Potato Rosti with
                                  Soy Emulsion and Chives 81

Cactus! . . . . Conchita Pibil 85

Captain Whidbey Inn, The . . . . . . Captain Whidbey's
                                  Penn Cove Ginger Mussels 89

Chateau Ste. Michelle . . . . Argentinean Style Mixed Grill 91

Entrées *continued*	**Recipe**	**Page**
Chuckanut Manor	Chuckanut Manor Crab Au Gratin	95
Coho Cafe	Applewood Smoked Salmon	97
Hunt Club (Sorrento Hotel)	Alaskan Halibut with Tagliatelle of Vegetables, Beurre Blanc and American Caviar	99
Kingfish Cafe, The	Macaroni and Cheese	103
Paradiso, Ristorante	Cannelloni di Fabrizio	105
Pasta & Co.	Chicken Baked in *Pasta & Co. Roasted Tomato Chutney Sauce*	111
Salish Lodge & Spa	Mint and Nut Crusted Rack of Lamb with Russian Banana Fingerling Potato Purée	113
Saluté of Bellevue	Italian Meatballs	117
SkyCity at the Needle (*Space Needle*)	Alderwood Smoked Salmon with Sushi Rice Cakes	119
Sostanza	Stuffed Pork Loin	121

Table of Contents

Table of Contents *continued*

Desserts	Recipe	Page
C Shop, The	Carmel Apples	125
Dahlia Lounge	White Chocolate Bread Pudding	127
Famous Northwest Catering Company, The	Vanilla Bean Cheesecake with Fresh Fruit Topping	131
Herbfarm, The	Lemon Verbena-Yogurt Panna Cotta	135
Macrina Bakery & Cafe	Cherry Almond Scones	137
Maltby Cafe, The	Maltby Cafe Marionberry Pie	141
Salish Lodge & Spa	Beignets and Chocolate Coffee Ice Cream	143
Savory Faire	Amaretto Bread Pudding	149
Sunflour Bakery & Cafe	Grand Marnier-Chocolate Cheesecake	151

Appendix · Page

Where to Find Special Ingredients	158
Store Directory	162
About the UW Alumnae Board	165
Credits	166
Special Thanks	167

Table of Contents

WASHINGTON STARS

Appetizers

Located on the 75th and 76th floors of the Bank of America Tower, the Columbia Tower Club is Seattle's premier business club. The Club offers business networking and social events to enrich and enhance the lives of its members and their families. Membership is by invitation via the sponsorship of an existing member in good standing.

Executive Chef, Kenneth McNamee, is an international award-winning chef. He has competed on two culinary Olympic teams. Ken has a passion for "exceeding Member's expectations." Whether it's a favorite dessert or an intimate dinner party, he truly makes "magic moments" for the Club's members and their guests.

COLUMBIA TOWER CLUB

The Columbia Tower Club
75th Floor
701 Fifth Ave
Seattle, WA 98104

206-622-2010

Seattle's premiere private business and social club

Please call for membership and private party information.

www.thecolumbiatowerclub.com

Sauté of Wild Mushrooms and Whipped Brie on Crostini

12 oz ripe Brie (chilled)
extra virgin olive oil
12 thin slices of baguette
12 oz sliced assorted mushrooms
1 tsp minced garlic
1/2 TBSP chopped parsley
salt
freshly ground black pepper

Remove the rind from the Brie. Put the Brie into a mixer with a paddle attachment and beat at medium speed for 5-10 minutes.

Rub the slices of baguette with olive oil and toast until they turn golden brown.

Pour a small amount of oil into a pan over medium heat. Wait for the pan to heat up and then add the mushrooms. Cook the mushrooms for a couple of minutes and then add the garlic and parsley. Sauté for a few minutes more until the mushrooms are cooked. Season with salt and freshly ground black pepper.

Lay out the slices of baguette and spread with whipped Brie. Top with mushrooms. If needed, add more salt and freshly ground black pepper.

DANIEL'S BROILER-LESCHI

Daniel's Broiler-Leschi
200 Lk Washington Blvd
Seattle, WA 98122

206-329-4191

Open 7 days a week

Happy Hour
4:30pm-6:30pm

Dinner
Sun-Thurs 5pm-10pm
Fri-Sat 5pm-11pm

Banquet facilities available

www.schwartzbros.com

Daniel's Leschi is the *original* Daniel's, and has been open for over 20 years. Open seven nights a week, Daniel's features 100% USDA Prime beef as well as fresh Northwest seafood.

Mike Dremann joined the Schwartz Brother's team over 10 years ago and has been Chef at the Leschi location for four years. Mike has become UW Football Coach Rick Nuehiesel's "Chef du Jour." Daniel's Leschi provides most of the meals during recruiting season—including breakfast at the restaurant, brunch at Rick's house and a prime rib buffet at the Don James Center.

Additional Daniel's Broilers are located on Lake Union and in downtown Bellevue.

Filet Strips Teriyaki

1/4 C vegetable oil
1 lb marinated tenderloin cubes
   (recipe below)
1/2 C reserved Teriyaki Sauce
minced green onions *(for garnish)*
toasted sesame seeds *(for garnish)*

Trim tenderloin of all excess fat. Cut into 3/4" cubes. Marinate in Teriyaki Sauce overnight in refrigerator.

Teriyaki Sauce Marinade

1-1/2 C soy sauce
1 C water
1 tsp fresh ground ginger
1 TBSP fresh minced garlic
1/8 C vegetable oil
1-1/4 C brown sugar
1/4 C minced green onions
1/4 C pineapple juice

Combine all ingredients and mix well. Reserve 1/2 C marinade for serving preparation **before adding meat**.

Next day, warm oil in sauté pan over medium-high heat. Drain tenderloin well and add to hot oil. Stir often to sear all sides. Add reserved Teriyaki Sauce and allow to reduce slightly.

Remove to serving tray. Sprinkle with green onions and seeds for garnish.

Serves 4 to 6

IL TERRAZZO CARMINE

Il Terrazzo Carmine
411 First Ave S
Seattle, WA 98104

206-467-7797

Lunch
Mon-Fri 11:30am-2:30pm

Dinner
Mon-Sat 5:30pm-10:30pm

Complimentary Valet Parking after 5pm on King Street

Il Terrazzo Carmine, owned and operated by Carmine Smeraldo for over 17 years, is one of Seattle's true dining anomalies— a highly successful restaurant with unfailingly high standards and a loyal sophisticated clientele. The cuisine has been acclaimed as Seattle's best by the media and more importantly, by local diners. Since 1984, Carmine Smeraldo's classic Italian restaurant has been where the locals have chosen to return over and over again.

Il Terrazzo Carmine is located in historic Pioneer Square. You'll find it nestled in an urban-renewed alley with entrances through the vintage lobby on First Ave or through the delightful courtyard in the back.

Calamari in Padella

1-1/2 lb calamari (cleaned and quartered)
2 TBSP olive oil
1 TBSP garlic
4 oz Sauce Prima Vera *(recipe below)*
1 TBSP Italian parsley (chopped)
2 TBSP lemon juice
salt and pepper to taste

In a large sauté pan, sauté the calamari in olive oil over high heat for 1 minute. Add garlic, Sauce Prima Vera and parsley. Sauté for an additional 3 minutes. Add lemon juice and salt and pepper to taste. Serve hot.

Sauce Prima Vera

1 can (16 oz) imported Italian tomatoes
4 cloves garlic
1/4 C olive oil
salt and pepper to taste
3 basil leaves

Cut tomatoes into julienne strips and place in bowl. Crush 4 cloves garlic and blanche in the olive oil. Add garlic mixture to the tomatoes. Add basil leaves. Salt and pepper to taste.

Serves 4

'O HANA

'O HANA
2207 1st Ave
Seattle, WA   98121

Phone: 206-956-9329

<u>Lunch</u>
Tues-Fri 11:30am-3pm
<u>Dinner</u>
7 nights a week
Early & late night Happy Hours

Reservations recommended

No Checks accepted

www.ohanabelltown.com

'O HANA is a 12-year dream come true for owner Kyle Yoshimura. After graduation from the UW with a degree in psychology, Kyle moved to Maui for a couple of years to be close to his retired dad and stepmom, a native of Molokai. He moved back to Seattle, staying in the service industry, where he built his " 'Ohana" (family). With the help of his family, 'O HANA was born.

'O HANA features a menu of island favorites: bento boxes, sushi in the bamboo lounge, pupus, robatas, lunch plates and weekly Hawaiian seafood specials....not to mention the "da kine" tropical drink menu.

From our 'O hana to your 'O hana, come visit us in the heart of Belltown.

Ahi Nori Tempura

12 oz Ahi tuna (#1 or #2 grade)
nori (seaweed) sheet
panko (Japanese bread crumbs)
tempura batter
　(which can be purchased in most stores)
oil *(for frying)*

Garlic Shoyu Sauce *(recipe below)*
Optional garnishes:
　gyoza skins
　sesame seeds
　julienne cucumbers

Cut Ahi into 1-1/2" to 2" strips and wrap nori sheet snuggly around. Dip in tempura batter. Generously bread with panko.

Deep fry for 20 seconds. Slice in 1/2" rounds. Cover with Garlic Shoyu Sauce *(recipe below)*.

Garnish with sliced fried gyoza skins, sesame seeds and julienne cucumbers.

Garlic Shoyu Sauce

8 oz shoyu (soy sauce)
5 oz sugar
1 oz rice vinegar
4 oz sesame oil

1 oz minced garlic
1/2 oz chili oil
1/2 oz canola oil

Serves 2

PALACE KITCHEN

The Palace Kitchen
2030 Fifth Ave
Seattle, WA 98121
206-448-2001

Open 7 nights a week
Serving full menu
5pm-1am
Cocktails until 2am

Reservations taken for parties of 6 OR MORE only

All major credit cards

www.tomdouglas.com

Tom Douglas, a Delaware native, has helped to define the Northwest style, or "Pacific Rim Cuisine," as it is sometimes called. Tom's creativity with local ingredients and his respect for Seattle's ethnic traditions have helped put his three restaurants on the national culinary map.

Tom and his wife, Jackie, opened the Palace Kitchen in March of 1996. The menu at the Palace features a more rustic style of cuisine, with a wood-fired grill offering nightly rotisserie specials. As much an up-scale bar as it is a restaurant, Palace Kitchen is a lively downtown favorite with Seattleites, serving a full menu until 1:00 am, seven nights a week.

Goat Cheese Fondue

At Palace Kitchen, we make our own fresh goat cheese which we use in this appetizer fondue. You could use any soft, mild, fresh goat cheese. It's fun to serve this in a fondue pot and surround it with chunks of grilled bread and crisp slices of apple for dunking.

2 C heavy cream
3 rounds (about 15 ounces)
    soft, fresh goat cheese*

freshly ground pepper
freshly ground nutmeg

Slowly warm the cream in a heavy saucepan over medium-low heat.

When the cream is warm, break the goat cheese into pieces and add it to the saucepan. Whisk until smooth.

Season to taste with black pepper and nutmeg. Pour into fondue pot and serve immediately.

* Depending on the particular goat cheese you use, you may need to use slightly more cheese or less cream. The fondue should be thick enough to coat a spoon.

Serves 6 to 8

RAY'S BOATHOUSE

Ray's Boathouse
6049 Seaview Ave NW
Seattle, WA 98107

206-789-3770

Open 7 days a week

Cafe
11:30am-10pm

Boathouse
5pm-9:30pm

www.rays.com

Regarded as a "must visit" by locals and travelers alike, Ray's Boathouse is famous for its impeccably fresh Northwest seafood. Ray's creates some of the finest cuisine in the Northwest and is a favorite spot for romantic dinners, meetings and special occasions.

Enjoy Ray's panoramic bayside view of Puget Sound and the Olympic Mountains. Every table—whether it is downstairs in the beautiful Boathouse dining room, upstairs in the more casual Cafe with its outdoor deck, or in one of our private banquet rooms—commands a spectacular view.

Ray's Boathouse Thai Mussels

- 1 C coconut milk
- 2 tsp fresh lime juice
- 1 tsp red curry paste
- 2 tsp Thai fish sauce
- 2/3 C sake
- 1 tsp minced garlic
- 1 tsp minced fresh ginger
- 1 tsp chopped fresh basil

- 2 lbs Penn Cove mussels *(cleaned and debearded)*
- 2-4 sprigs basil *(for garnish)*

In a large bowl, mix all ingredients **(except the mussels and basil)** with a wire whip to create the broth.

Heat a heavy saucepan over high heat for about 30 seconds. Add mussels and broth. Bring to a boil and reduce heat. Cover with lid and simmer for about 5 minutes or until mussels fully open.

Divide mussels into bowls and serve with broth and plenty of crusty bread.

Tip: *To ensure the safety and quality of the shellfish, make sure mussels are alive and shells are closed. Always purchase from a reputable fishmonger.*

Serves 4 as an appetizer or 2 as an entrée.

ROY'S SEATTLE

Roy's Seattle
1900 Fifth Avenue
Seattle, WA 98101
(located in the Westin Hotel)

206-256-7697

Breakfast
Mon-Fri 6am-10:30am
Sat-Sun 6am-11:30am

Lunch
Daily 11:30am-2pm

Dinner
Nightly 5pm-10pm

Roy's Seattle is an upscale Euro-Asian kitchen utilizing fresh, local ingredients; and is part of internationally acclaimed Chef Roy Yamaguchi's prestigious family of restaurants.

Our menu changes daily with offerings of "Dim Sum Style-Appetizers" such as Crisp Chinatown Chicken Spring Rolls, or Applewood Grilled Szechwan Style Baby Back Ribs. In our "Fresh Salads" section of the menu, you will frequently find Hibachi Grilled Thai Chicken Salad or Vine Ripened Tomato and Mozzarella Cheese. Entrees might include Bamboo Steamed Chilean Sea Bass or Garlic Parmesan Crusted Lamb Shank.

Northwest Salmon Satay with Maui Onion Dipping Sauce

6 oz King Salmon *(cut into 1/2" squares)*
6" bamboo skewers
sesame seeds
3 oz mixed baby lettuces
pickled red ginger

Cut up the salmon and marinate in the Marinade *(below)* for 2 hours.

Marinade

1/4 C brown sugar
1/8 C soy sauce *(cut with an equal amount of water)*
pinch of crushed red chiles
1 tsp sesame oil

When marinated, carefully skewer the salmon onto bamboo and sprinkle with sesame seeds. Barbecue or pan cook on low heat until "medium." Do not overcook.

On a plate, arrange baby mixed greens and salmon skewers. Top with pickled ginger. Serve with Maui Onion Sauce *(recipe next page)*.

(continued on next page)

ROY'S SEATTLE

Roy's Seattle
1900 Fifth Avenue
Seattle, WA 98101
(located in the Westin Hotel)

206-256-7697

Breakfast
Mon-Fri 6am-10:30am
Sat-Sun 6am-11:30am

Lunch
Daily 11:30am-2pm

Dinner
Nightly 5pm-10pm

Top off your meal with Roy's signature dessert, "Melting Hot Chocolate Souffle."

Come join us for a taste treat you will remember.

Two-hour validated parking is provided through the Westin Hotel Parking Garage located off Westlake Avenue in downtown Seattle.

Northwest Salmon Satay
with Maui Onion Dipping Sauce *continued*

Maui Onion Dipping Sauce

1 large sweet Maui onion	1/4 C water
(or a comparable sweet onion in season)	1/4 C soy sauce
1/2 C rice wine vinegar	1/8 C canola oil

In a food processor, pulp the onion. Add all ingredients **except the oil**. Blend together.

On low speed, slowly add the oil until it is emulsified. This sauce can be made far in advance. It will keep in the refrigerator up to 2 weeks.

Serves 3

SAN CARLOS RESTAURANT

San Carlos Restaurant
279 Madison Ave
Bainbridge Island, WA 98110

206-842-1999

Open 7 days a week
from 5pm to 9:30pm

Reservations Recommended

Visa & MC accepted

San Carlos Restaurant

San Carlos Restaurant opened in May of 1984, and has had a wonderful eighteen-year run as a free-standing restaurant and catering company. It's one of the first Northwestern spots to introduce a decidedly South-western influence to the style, flavors, colors and textures of Mexican food. Their custom smoked offerings and seafood selections, award-winning entrees and fresh specials prepared daily are sure to delight.

San Carlos Salsa

One 28 oz can fire roasted tomatoes
One 28 oz can diced tomatoes
One 28 oz can crushed & concentrated tomato paste
1-1/2 large yellow onions
4 TBSP salt
4 TBSP fresh puréed garlic
2 or 3 TBSP ground cumin
3 or 4 medium-sized fresh jalapeños
1 medium-sized bunch of cilantro
1/4 C white wine vinegar

Place fire roasted tomatoes in food processor and purée. Add diced and crushed tomatoes and processed tomatoes in a mixing bowl. Peel one onion, cube and place in blender bowl. Add salt, garlic and cumin to blender bowl and purée. Add purée to mixing bowl.

Wash and stem jalapeños. Cut in half, finely dice and add to mix. Wash cilantro and chop well. Mince remaining half onion and add to mix. Stir mixture and add white wine vinegar.

Salsa will stay fresh for 2-3 days in refrigerator. Thin with a little water if salsa becomes too thick.

(continued on next page)

SAN CARLOS RESTAURANT

San Carlos Restaurant
279 Madison Ave
Bainbridge Island, WA
98110

206-842-1999

Open 7 days a week
from 5pm to 9:30pm

Reservations Recommended

Visa & MC accepted

San Carlos

Open seven days a week from 5.00 pm, the restaurant is located on Bainbridge Island which is 35 minutes from Seattle by Washington State Ferry. Call 206-842-1999 for local directions. San Carlos is within walking distance from the Bainbridge Ferry Terminal. The trip over from Seattle is a refreshing and exciting escape from the city for a day or an easy way to entertain out-of-town vistors.

Come visit San Carlos soon!

San Carlos Salsa *continued*

This traditional salsa may be used as the base for any number of delicious adaptions and variations.

For a wonderful creamy salsa sauce that is delicious with chicken, seafood or salads, add fresh mayonnaise, sour cream, plus a little salt, garlic and white pepper to taste.

You may also thin the salsa somewhat and add black beans, Kalamata olives, avocado, artichoke hearts, goat cheese, etc… to make an exotic and superb dip for chips and party appetizers.

You can also heat 1/2 lb butter with a cup of the San Carlos Salsa. As the butter melts and the salsa warms, it will blend nicely. Add white wine. A chardonnay will flavor but not sweeten the sauce and is delicious for sautéing prawns or scampi. The prawns will sauté quickly in this very simple-to-prepare dish. Garnish your sautéed prawns with some goat cheese and some grated Asiago (or other hard Italian cheese) and serve with a warmed baguette. (Your guests will be eating from the palm of your hand.)

This sauce is also a wonderful topping for other grilled fish, fowl or beef.

SEASTAR RESTAURANT & RAW BAR

Seastar Restaurant
& Raw Bar
205 108th Ave NE
Bellevue, WA 98004

425-456-0010

Lunch
Mon-Fri: 11:30am-2:30pm

Dinner
Mon-Sat 5pm-10pm
Sun 5pm-9pm

Raw Bar
Mon-Fri: 11:30am-Closing
Sat-Sun 5pm-Closing

www.seastarrestaurant.com

Chef John Howe was born in Chicago, moved to Seattle in the late 1960's and in the mid-seventies began his culinary career in Seattle at the age of 15. He has since worked for many of Seattle's finest restaurants, working his way from the typical starting position of dishwasher to prep cook, line cook, sous chef and then chef. John has been recognized as one of Seattle's premier chefs by the James Beard Foundation.

On March 11, 2002 John opened Seastar Restaurant and Raw Bar in Bellevue, WA. Seastar offers fresh fish and seafood from the Pacific Northwest, Hawaii, South Pacific and South America as well as center cut, corn fed, 28-day aged Nebraska steaks, great pastas, poultry and salads.

Halibut Ceviche with Pico de Gallo Relish

1 lb fresh halibut (cut into 1" cubes)
4 TBSP fresh lime juice
4 TBSP fresh lemon juice
2 TBSP tomato juice
1/2 tsp black pepper (freshly ground)
1/2 tsp salt
1/8 tsp tabasco sauce
1/2 C tomato (seeded and diced 1/4")

1/4 C ripe tomatillo (diced 1/4")
1-1/2 tsp fresh jalapeño (seeded and minced)
2 TBSP cilantro (chopped coarse)
1 TBSP olive oil
1 avocado (diced 1/4")

4 cilantro sprigs *(as garnish)*
4 fresh lime squeezes *(as garnish)*

Mix the juices with the salt and pepper until well blended. Add the halibut and marinate for a minimum of 5 hours. (Up to a maximum of 10-12 hours).
Refrigerate while marinating.

Drain the halibut and toss together with the remaining ingredients **except the cilantro sprigs and lime squeeze.** Place the ceviche on the plates and garnish with the cilantro springs and lime squeezes.

Serve with cracker bread (such as black pepper croccantini) or tortilla chips.

Serves 6 to 8

SKYCITY AT THE NEEDLE

SkyCity at the Needle
203 6th Ave N
Seattle, WA 98109-5005

206-905-2100

Hours of operation vary
seasonally

All Major Cards Accepted

www.spaceneedle.com

Take in the splendor of the Puget Sound area from SkyCity, the Space Needle's "all-new" revolving restaurant. Located 500 feet above Seattle, SkyCity features many exclusive and signature menu items and celebrates Pacific Northwest cuisine with freshness and dazzling flavor prepared by Chef Gerard Bengle.

The decor is 1960's retro inspired; however, the mood is distinctively modern. Breathtaking views are guaranteed from all tables. Your elevator ride and Observation Deck visit are complimentary when dining at SkyCity. Join us for lunch, dinner, or weekend brunch.

SkyCity Crab Cakes with Curry Aïoli and Apple Salsa

Crab Cakes

- 1 lb Dungeness crabmeat
- 1 C heavy cream (reduced by 2/3)
- 1 TBSP Dijon mustard
- 1 tsp chopped garlic
- 1/2 diced jalepeño pepper
- 1 tsp Old Bay Seasoning
- 1/2 C oven roasted corn kernels
- 1 C Japanese style bread crumbs *(plus additional crumbs to coat crab cakes)*
- clarified butter to sauté crabcakes *(enough to coat 1/16" on the bottom of the pan)*

Drain crabmeat and press to remove as much moisture as possible. Combine all ingredients *except bread crumbs for coating and clarified butter.* **Refrigerate overnight uncovered.** To form crab cakes, roll into 2 oz balls. Roll in additional Japanese bread crumbs just prior to cooking.

Curry Aïoli

- 1/2 C mayonnaise
- 1 TBSP water
- 1 clove garlic (very finely chopped)
- pinch of ground white pepper
- 1/2 teaspoon mild curry powder

Combine all ingredients. **Refrigerate overnight.**

(continued on next page)

SKYCITY AT THE NEEDLE

SkyCity at the Needle
203 6th Ave N
Seattle, WA 98109-5005

206-905-2100

Hours of operation vary seasonally

All Major Cards Accepted

www.spaceneedle.com

Jeffrey J. Wright serves as Chairman of the Board of Directors for the Space Needle. He and his family have been owners of the Seattle Landmark since its construction in 1962 for the World's Fair.

Mr. Wright is a graduate of the University of Washington with a degree in construction management. Wright's vast experience in the real estate development and construction management arenas has won him several awards.

Wright is a member of the University of Washington Alumni Association, and both the University of Washington and Seattle University President's Clubs.

SkyCity Crab Cakes with Apple Salsa and Curry Aïoli *continued*

Apple Salsa

- 2 Braeburn or Fuji apples *(depending upon season)*
- 1 TBSP onion (chopped)
- 1 TBSP red bell pepper (diced)
- 1 TBSP parsley (chopped)
- 1 TBSP cilantro (chopped)
- 2 TBSP light vinaigrette
- cilantro sprigs *(for garnish)*

Julienne the apples. Mix all salsa ingredients together.

Crab Cake Preparation

Place a sauté pan over medium high heat. Add clarified butter. Sauté formed crab cakes until brown on both sides.

Place the Apple Salsa in a mound on a serving plattter. Lay crab cakes on top. Drizzle with the Curry Aïoli. Garnish with cilantro sprigs.

Serves 6 to 8

SWEET ADDITION

Sweet Addition has been creating exceptional pastries, desserts and Northwest fare for over seventeen years. Their commitment to fresh, whole ingredients and their passion for truly great cooking continues to inspire both locals and visitors.

Located in Issaquah's historic Gilman Village and, now in the new Issaquah Highlands, Sweet Addition offers "sweet," delicious and casual dining, Northwest High Teas, executive catering and box lunches.

Sweet Addition

Gilman Village
317 NW Gilman Blvd
"Sweet" 43
Issaquah, WA 98027

425-392-5661

★

Issaquah Highlands
1927 15th Avenue NE
Issaquah, WA 98029

425-427-8766

Asparagus, Prosciutto & Basil Aïoli on Baguette

2 bunches asparagus
  (blanched and cooled)
1 lb prosciutto *(thinly sliced)*

6-8 Roma tomatoes
  (sliced horizontally)
Basil Aïoli *(see recipe below)*

Basil Aïoli

4 egg yolks
1 TBSP Dijon mustard
3 TBSP white wine vinegar
4 cloves garlic

1-1/2 C olive oil
1/2 C canola oil
salt and pepper
1 bunch chopped basil leaves

Combine egg yolks, mustard, vinegar and garlic in food processor. Gradually add oils—very slowly at first. When thickened, add salt, pepper and basil.

Store in refrigerator for 2 days. Generously spread Aïoli onto baguettes. Add asparagus, prosciutto and sliced Romas.

Wrap in foil, throw in your Husky cooler, head to the game and enjoy!

Serves 8

TOSONI'S RESTAURANT

Tosoni's Restaurant
& Catering
14320 NE 20th
Bellevue, WA 98007

425-644-1668

Dinner
Tue-Sat 5pm-10:30pm
Closed Sun & Mon

All major credit cards

Walter Walcher is the Eastside's best-known Austrian-born and trained chef. Graduating from the Culinary Institute of Villach, Walcher opened Tosoni's in 1983. This little bistro quickly became the Bellevue *Insiders'* favorite gourmand establishment.

Tosoni's is always full of the repeat customers that feel as though they have become part of his extended family. The white starched tablecloths and the European ambience all add to the experience, and you soon feel as though you have made a cross-Atlantic journey.

Portabello Mushroom Appetizer

"One of my most popular appetizers, this is a simple and tasty start to any meal."—Walter

2 large Portabello mushrooms (stemless)
1/2 C soy sauce
1 C water
1 C all-purpose flour *(for dredging)*
5 C vegetable oil

low sodium citrus soy sauce *(to taste)*
   (can be found at Uwajimaya Stores)
1-1/2 tsp sesame oil
pinch of sesame seeds

Cut mushrooms into 3/4" wide strips.

Dip into mixture of soy sauce and water.

Roll mushrooms in flour until they are well coated.

Fry mushrooms in hot (385 degrees) vegetable oil until they are crisp and golden (approximately 2 minutes).

Top with a mixture of citrus soy sauce and sesame oil. Garnish with a pinch of sesame seeds.

Serves 4

WASHINGTON STARS

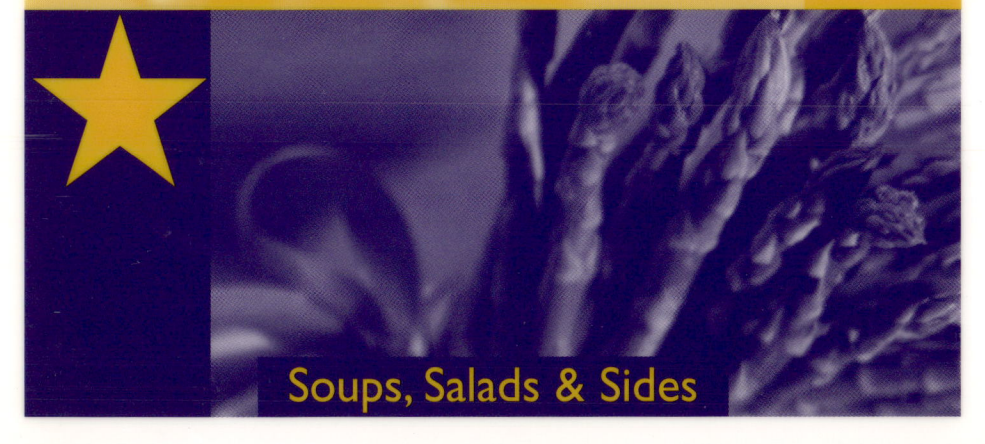

Soups, Salads & Sides

12TH AVENUE CAFE

12th Avenue Cafe
775-G NW Gilman Blvd
Issaquah, WA 98027
(located in the Issaquah Commons)

425-392-5975

Hours
Mon–Tue   6am-3pm
Wed-Fri   6am-8pm
Sat   7am-8pm
Sun   8am-8pm

The number of "Best Breakfast" awards bestowed on the 12th Avenue Cafe are too numerous to list. Basics are the specialty there and the food is delicious.

With a move from 12th Avenue in Issaquah to the Issaquah Commons in 1995, their original wonderful breakfasts remain unchanged. Reservations are not accepted, but once you put your name on the list at the door, the wait isn't too long and the breakfast, available all day, is always worth waiting for.

The Montana Special is their signature item and it's enough to fill you for all day. If you want a home cooked meal—breakfast, lunch or dinner—served hot and service with a smile, the 12th Avenue Cafe is the place!

Dragon Soup

Bring the following ingredients to a boil.

- 4 quarts of water
- 6 cubes beef bouillon
- 2 TBSP cumin
- 2 TBSP chili powder
- 1 TBSP granulated garlic
- 1 package taco mix
- 1 TBSP crushed red chilies
- 1 tsp cayenne pepper

Once the above ingredients come to a boil, add the following:

- 1 C uncooked white rice
- 1/2 pulled chicken (cooked and de-boned)
- 1 baby back pork rib loin (cooked and pulled)
- 1 C toasted, sliced almonds
- 2 TBSP toasted sesame seeds
- 1/2 stock celery (diced)
- 1 medium onion
- 1 green bell pepper (diced)
- 1/2 lb mushrooms (sliced)

Then, bring to a boil over high heat again. Reduce heat to medium and simmer covered for five minutes. Water can be added for desired consistency.

Makes approximately 16 cups

ALLIGATOR PEAR

Alligator Pear
2523 Fifth Avenue
Seattle, WA 98121

206-728-5897

Located at the corner of
Fifth Avenue and Vine Street

Hours
Lunch and Dinner Served
Mon-Fri: 10am-7:30pm

Alligator Pear serves sandwiches, soups and salads made fresh daily from quality, seasonal ingredients. In addition they serve specialty sodas, beer, wine and espresso.

The owners (one, a native of Albuquerque, New Mexico, who trained at the Culinary Institute of America; the other, a Seattle native and UW alumna) bring a combined nineteen years of experience working with food to Alligator Pear.

"We love having a small, neighborhood sandwich shop and providing something of quality that is accessible every weekday. We are often asked what makes our food so good. We tell them it's the ingredients. We love to make common ingredients exceed ordinary expectations."

Roasted Tomato Soup

We like to serve this soup with a seeded baguette from Grand Central Bakery, or a grilled cheese sandwich with asparagus and white cheddar.

- 5 lbs tomatoes (quartered)
- 3 celery stalks and tops (medium diced)
- 2 carrots (peeled and medium diced)
- 1 large onion (sliced)
- 5 cloves garlic (crushed)
- 4 sprigs fresh thyme (take the thyme leaves off the sprigs)
- 1/4 C extra virgin olive oil
- salt and pepper to taste
- 5 to 10 leaves fresh basil *(optional)*

Place tomatoes, celery, carrots, onion, garlic and thyme in a 9"x13" roasting pan. Coat the tomatoes and the rest of the ingredients with the olive oil. Roast in a 375-degree oven until all the ingredients are broken down and soft enough to purée. (Approximately 1 to 1-1/2 hours.)

Place the ingredients in a blender and purée until smooth. If it is too thick, add water, vegetable stock or chicken stock to thin. Five to ten leaves of fresh basil can be added at this time for additional flavor.

Warm soup and serve.

Serves 4 to 6

THE CALCUTTA GRILL

The Calcutta Grill
15500 Six Penny Lane
Newcastle, WA 98059

425-793-4646

Brunch
Sun 10am–2pm

Lunch
Mon-Sat 11am–5pm

Happy Hour
Mon-Fri 3pm–6pm

Dinner
Nightly 5pm–10pm

Reservations recommended

www.newcastlegolf.com

The Calcutta Grill is the primary restaurant at The Golf Club at Newcastle, Seattle's ultimate golf club. The Golf Club features breathtaking panoramic views of Mt. Rainier, the Olympics and the Cascades. When you dine at The Calcutta Grill you can enjoy both the view as well as the superb culinary skills of Joel Droba, executive chef.

Droba, a Chicago native, previously served as executive sous chef at the Bellevue Club in Bellevue, WA; and as banquet chef for Noble House Hotels.

Joel's extensive banquet background is ideal since The Calcutta Grill and its banquet facilities are also a perfect location for corporate events and weddings.

Goat Cheese Scallion Spoon Bread

- 1 lb large cubed sourdough bread (crust included)
- 1/4 C roasted garlic
- 1/2 lb goat cheese crumbles
- 1 bunch julienne scallions
- 1 quart heavy cream
- 1/4 lb butter
- 3 whole eggs
- 1 tsp salt
- 1/2 tsp black pepper

In a saucepan, scald cream, garlic and butter.

In a bowl, crack eggs and then temper eggs with cream mixture. *(To temper, slowly add the hot cream to the eggs while whisking. This will help keep the temperature even.)*

In a large bowl, add all the ingredients together and mix thoroughly. The mixture should appear a little "liquid."

Place in a bread loaf pan and bake in a 350-degree oven for 45 minutes or until an internal temperature of 160 degrees is reached.

Serves 6

CANLIS

Canlis
2576 Aurora Ave N
Seattle, WA 98109

206-283-3313

Hours
Mon-Sat Dinner only
5:30pm-midnight

Reservations recommended

www.canlis.com

Canlis is not just the name of the famous restaurant but of a famous Seattle family. Today the third generation runs the restaurant whose roots go back to a Greek immigrant named Nick Canlis who came to the United States through Ellis Island in 1908. He worked his way across the country and started a simple cafe in California in the 1920's. His son, Peter, (pictured left) became his apprentice.

In the late 1930's, Peter struck out on his own heading to Hawaii to sell dry goods. During WWII, Peter's knowledge of food and shrewd purchasing skills led to an offer to manage the United Services Organization in Hololulu. Soon everyone on Oahu knew that the best meal to be had was at the USO!

In 1950, Peter moved to Seattle and opened Canlis. Today, 52 years later, it is run by the third generation of restaurateurs, Chris and Alice Canlis.

Canlis Salad

(For each serving)

- 1/4 head Romaine lettuce (washed and cut into 1" pieces)
- 3 wedges Roma tomato
- 3 TBSP croutons *(recipe follows)*
- 2 TBSP chopped green onion
- 2 TBSP well-done, chopped bacon (drained)
- 1 tsp dried oregano leaves (crumbled)
- 3 TBSP freshly grated Romano cheese
- 2 TBSP *(or to taste)* fresh mint (finely chopped)
- Kosher salt *(to taste)*
- freshly ground black pepper *(to taste)*
- 1 oz *(or to taste)* Canlis Salad Dressing *(recipe follows)*
- 1 Parmesan Crisp *(recipe follows)*

In a large, well-seasoned wooden salad bowl, combine Romaine, tomato wedges, croutons, green onion, bacon, oregano, half the Romano cheese, half the mint and a generous sprinkling of kosher salt and freshly ground black pepper.

Toss the salad dry to distribute the ingredients evenly, then pour on dressing and toss again. Transfer half the salad to plates and then rest a Parmesan crisp *(recipe follows)* against the dressed greens. Put the remaining salad on the plate, securing the crisp in an upright position. Finish with remaining Romano cheese, remaining mint, and a generous grind of black pepper.

(continued on next page)

CANLIS

Canlis
2576 Aurora Ave N
Seattle, WA 98109

206-283-3313

Hours
Mon-Sat Dinner only
5:30pm-midnight

Reservations recommended

www.canlis.com

Executive Chef Greg Atkinson's contemporary Northwest cuisine follows the seasons. By reinventing classic Canlis dishes, Greg has made it the best place to dine in 2002.

When not at Canlis, Greg can be found at the Puget Sound Environmental Learning Center (PSELC) on Bainbridge Island. As Chef at PSELC, Atkinson creates the menus for a series of educational programs that incorporate science, technology and the arts.

A prolific writer, Atkinson is the author of *In Season* and *The Northwest Essentials Cookbook*. He is a contributing editor to *Food Arts Magazine*, and a regular contributor to *Pacific Northwest Magazine* and *The Seattle Times*. The James Beard Foundation awarded Atkinson the M.K. Fisher Distinguished Writing Award in 2000.

Canlis Salad *continued*

Seasoned Croutons
(Makes about 4 cups)

1/4 C butter (1/2 stick)
1 TBSP salt
1 TBSP dried oregano
1 TBSP dried "Italian seasoning" blend
1 tsp freshly ground black pepper
1 tsp granulated garlic
4 C European-style white bread
   (cut into 1/4" cubes)

Preheat oven to 300 degrees. (Convection oven is ideal.) Melt butter and add salt, dried oregano, "Italian seasoning," pepper and garlic. Toss the seasoned melted butter with bread cubes.

Bake in preheated oven, stirring every 5 minutes for 30-40 minutes, or until crisp and golden brown. Cool completely at room temperature before serving or storing.

You may keep extra croutons in an airtight container at room temperature for several days.

(continued on next page)

Canlis Salad *continued*

Parmesan Cheese Crisps
(Makes 12)

12 oz Parmesan cheese
   (grated into long strands)

2 TBSP olive oil
2 TBSP flour

Preheat oven to 400 degrees. Line 2 baking sheets with parchment cooking paper and brush with olive oil.

Sprinkle parchment with flour and shake off the excess. Sprinkle rounded table-spoons full of grated cheese in six-inch circles on the prepared baking sheets.

Bake 7-10 minutes or until golden brown. Cool and carefully remove crisps from parchment. Serve at room temperature.

Crisps may be made up to 24 hours in advance and kept loosely covered at room temperature.

(continued below)

Canlis Salad *continued*

Canlis Salad Dressing
(Makes about 1 C to serve 8)

1 egg (coddled*)
1/4 C freshly squeezed lemon juice

1 tsp freshly ground black pepper
1/2 C olive oil

* To coddle an egg: Place cold egg in a small container of warm water. In pan on stove, heat to boiling enough water to cover the egg. With a spoon, gently immerse the egg into the boiling water. Remove the pan from the heat. Cover and let stand for 30 seconds. Immediately put the egg in a containter of cold water to cool.

In a small bowl, beat the coddled egg with lemon juice.

While still beating, stream in olive oil. Add black pepper and continue beating for a few seconds to create a smooth dressing.

THE CAPTAIN WHIDBEY INN

The Captain Whidbey Inn
2072 W Capt Whidbey Inn Rd
Coupeville, WA 98239

360-678-4097
Toll-free: 800-366-4097

Owned by Captain John Colby Stone

Activities include golf, sea-kyaking, horseback riding, and sailing on Capt. Stone's 52' ketch "Cutty Sark."

Checks and All Major Credit Cards

www.captainwhidbey.com

The
Captain Whidbey
Inn

The Captain Whidbey Inn has been offering outstanding lodging, food and drink from the wooded shore of Penn Cove since 1907. Quaint rooms in the historic main building and luxurious cabins and cottages feature featherbeds and warm down comforters.

The Inn's dining room features an exquisite view of Penn Cove in a warm, rustic setting. The fare is classic country inn with a North-west flavor. Abundant fresh sea-foods, world-famous Penn Cove mussels, *(see recipe on page 90)* fresh herbs and vegetables from private gardens all contribute to an excellent regional reputation.

Steven Clarke stands 6' 7" in his tiny kitchen. He worked in Alaska as a Commercial Fisherman to pay for his education in the Culinary Arts prior to coming to The Inn as Chef.

Tomato Basil Vinaigrette

2-1/2 C olive oil
1 C (firmly packed) fresh basil (finely chopped)
1 C balsamic vinegar
1 TBSP shallots
1 tsp seasoning salt
1 tsp garlic
2 C Roma tomatoes (puréed)
2 C rehydrated sundried tomatoes (puréed separately from Romas)
spinach leaves *(serving size depends on personal preference)*
goat cheese *(optional garnish)*
toasted pecans *(optional garnish)*

Place all ingredients **(except Roma tomatoes, sundried tomatoes and optional garnishes)** in a mixer/blender and purée.

In a large bowl, mix together the Roma and sundried tomato purées.

Slowly add the blended mixture to the tomato purée. Pour into a non-metal container. *(May be stored up to 8 or 9 days in the refrigerator.)*

To serve, toss fresh-washed spinach leaves with the dressing and garnish with a bit of goat cheese and toasted pecans. (Use approximately 4 oz dressing per serving of salad.)

Makes 2 quarts *(Approximately 16 servings)*

CHUCKANUT MANOR

Chuckanut Manor
Restaurant and B&B
3056 Chuckanut Dr
Bow, WA 98232

360-766-6191

Sunday Brunch 10:30am
Lunch Tues-Sat 11:30am
Dinner Tues-Thurs & Sat 3pm
Friday Seafood Smorgy 5pm
Closed Mondays
All major credit cards

www.chuckanutmanor.com

The "Manor" has been serving the Northwest for over 35 years. Under the direction of Pat Woolcock, a 1970 UW graduate, and Chef Margarito Brito, the "Manor" provides a variety of dining experiences in a setting that overlooks Samish Bay and the San Juan Islands. The Friday Smorgy is outstanding and the Brunch is award-winning. Stay over at the Bed and Breakfast for a full "Manor" experience.

For more information, their menu, etc... check out their website.

Directions:
Located south of Bellingham
Northbound on I-5, from Seattle:
Exit 231
(Chuckanut Dr./Bow-Edison)
The drive is well worth it!

Broccoli Salad

Dressing

- 1 whole egg
- 1 egg yolk
- 1/2 C sugar
- 1 tsp dry mustard
- 1/2 TBSP cornstarch
- 1/4 C white vinegar
- 2 TBSP butter
- 1/2 C mayonnaise

In medium-sized bowl, whisk together whole egg, egg yolk, sugar, dry mustard and cornstarch. In a saucepan, bring vinegar to a boil. Whisk in egg mixture. Cook for 1 minute or until thickened. Remove from heat. Add butter and mayonnaise. Let chill for 1 hour.

Salad Preparation

- 4 C raw broccoli (chopped in 1/2" pieces)
- 1 C raisins
- 1 C sliced mushrooms
- 6 slices bacon (cooked, then crumbled)
- 1 medium onion (diced) *(optional)*

Combine broccoli, raisins, mushrooms, bacon and onion after Dressing has chilled. Pour dressing over salad and toss lightly.

Serves 4

EARTH & OCEAN

Earth & Ocean
1112 Fourth Ave
Seattle, WA 98101
(Located in the W Hotel)

206-264-6060

Breakfast
Mon-Fri 6:30am-10:30am
Sat-Sun 7:30am-11:30am

Lunch
Mon-Fri 11:30am-2:30pm

Dinner
Nightly 5pm

www.myriadrestaurantgroup.com

Johnathan Sundstrom took the culinary lead as Executive Chef at Earth & Ocean restaurant, Sept. 1, 2000. Within six months at his post, *Food and Wine Magazine* named him one of the "Top Ten Best New Chefs" at their 14th annual award presentations, *Best New Chefs in America for 2001*. He provides a contemporary American menu at Earth & Ocean that has enticed and impressed locals, as well as business travelers and visitors. He has developed a culinary aesthetic style through his fifteen years of experience and study of Japanese, Latin and European cuisine.

John's current ambitions are to explore regional and American foods and merge them with his vision for an ever-changing menu.

Warm, Truffled Asparagus with Aged Gouda and Endive

32 pc. jumbo asparagus
   (trimmed, bottom 1/3 peeled,
   blanched and shocked)
4 oz truffle butter*

kosher or sea salt
fresh ground black pepper
white truffle oil*
chives (sliced thin)

Warm asparagus with truffle butter, salt, pepper and truffle oil. Divide equally onto serving plates and sprinkle with chives.

4 oz aged Gouda
   (organic from Sammish Bay), shaved
1 head frisee* (torn into bite-sized
   pieces, washed and spun dry)
1 head Belgian endive (sliced thin)

4 oz arugula (washed and spun dry)
1 lemon (juiced)
2 TBSP extra virgin olive oil
kosher or sea salt
fresh ground black pepper

Toss greens with lemon juice, olive oil, salt and pepper. Mound over warm asparagus. Shave Gouda over each portion of greens and serve.

Serves 4 to 6   *see Appendix*

FLEMING'S PRIME
STEAKHOUSE & WINE BAR

Fleming's Prime Steakhouse
& Wine Bar
1001 Third Ave
Seattle, WA 98104

206-587-5300

Lunch
Mon-Fri 11:30am-2pm
Dinner
Nightly 5pm-10pm

All major credit cards

Fleming's Prime Steakhouse and Wine Bar has all the resources necessary to assist Chef Christopher Gardner in creating a menu selection fitting for a great steakhouse. All prime beef is cut in-house daily including porterhouse, T-bones and specialty cuts. Fleming's also offers a wide range of entrees other than steak and wonderful desserts. The wine list consists of 100 wines by the glass as well as a reserve list.

Chef Gardner is a Washington state native originally from Walla Walla. He honed his culinary skills while living throughout the Pacific Northwest.

Barbecue Cajun Shrimp

- 1 lb shrimp
- 1 tsp minced garlic
- 1 tsp cayenne pepper
- 1 tsp paprika
- 1 tsp black pepper
- 1 tsp tabasco
- 1 tsp Worcestershire Sauce
- 1 oz corn oil
- 1/2 jalepeño pepper (diced)

Clean and de-vein shrimp.

Combine all ingredients and marinate shrimp 3 hours in the refrigerator.

Sauté just before serving.

This is great served warm with your favorite rice or on a salad.

Serves 4 to 6 *(depending on size of shrimp)*

GILBERT'S ON MAIN

Gilbert's on Main
10024 Main St
Old Bellevue, WA 98004

425-455-5650

Hours
Mon-Fri 7am-3pm
Sat-Sun 8am-3pm

Gilbert's Main Street Bagel Deli

In the spirit of the great delicatessens of New York and Los Angeles, Steve Gilbert has created a hip, stylish and fun deli in the heart of Bellevue. Marble-top bistro tables and ornately painted walls add to the ambience.

Gilbert's on Main is the perfect place to come in to get your morning paper (*New York Times* or *Financial Times of London*, to name a few) and enjoy cafe society in romantic Old Bellevue.

If you haven't experienced Gilbert's for the best breakfast or lunch in Bellevue, don't you think it's time?

Apple Walnut Gorgonzola Salad

Caramelized Walnuts
4 C walnuts (raw)
4 TBSP butter
1/3 C granulated sugar
1-1/2 oz maple syrup
1-1/2 oz cooking sherry

In a large sauté pan on medium heat, melt the butter. Add walnuts and stir thoroughly to coat completely. Add sugar and stir until melted onto walnuts. Add maple syrup and stir. Add sherry and stir. Continue sautéing until sherry is reduced. Transfer to sheet pan and allow to cool.

Apple Cider Vinaigrette
1 C canola oil
1 C Heinz apple cider vinegar
1/2 C granulated sugar
1/8 C DaVinci Apple Syrup*
1 tsp salt

Combine ingredients in a mixing bowl and whisk briskly with a wire whip. Dressing will need to be whisked well again before adding to salad.

(continued on next page)   *see Appendix

GILBERT'S ON MAIN

Gilbert's on Main
10024 Main St
Old Bellevue, WA 98004

425-455-5650

Hours
Mon-Fri 7am-3pm
Sat-Sun 8am-3pm

The Biggest Portions West of
New York City!

★

You Say Pastrami...
We Say How High?

★

Matzo Ball Soup...
Such a Matzo Ball!

★

You Buy the Sandwich...
We'll Throw in the Bread.

★

Winner!!!

Seattle Times Readers Poll:

★ Best Business Lunch

★ Best Breakfast

★ Best Brunch

Apple Walnut Gorgonzola Salad *continued*

Salad Preparation

3 med-sized heads of green leaf lettuce
6 red delicious apples
   (cut into 1/2" cubes)
4 C Caramelized Walnuts
3 C Gorgonzola cheese
   (coarsely crumbled)
Gilbert's Apple Cider Vinaigrette
red onion (thinly sliced) *(for garnish)*

Place washed and chopped greens in a large salad bowl. Add desired amount of well-whisked vinaigrette, and toss lightly to coat greens.

In a large bowl, mix cubed apples, caramelized walnuts and coarsely crumbled Gorgonzola cheese.

Pile individual plates with greens and top with apple-walnut-Gorgonzola mixture.

Garnish with a few strands of red onion.

Serves 6 to 8

JUANITA BAY
SPORTS PUB AND EATERY

Juanita Bay Sports Pub
and Eatery
9736 NE 120th Place
Kirkland, WA 98034

425-823-6402

No reservations needed

Open daily at 11am
Weekend breakfast at 9am
Full Bar
Outside dining and
sand volleyball court

Credit cards accepted

"Our goal is to provide you with more than just a Sports Pub and Eatery. We want to provide you with a warm friendly hangout, where you can enjoy good beverages and high quality, good tasting at reasonable prices.

"Let us cater your next party. Allow us to prepare a special experience for you to enjoy here or at your home, office, boat, wedding or anywhere. We offer full service coordination of special events...large or small, and will deliver a catered affair beyond your expectations."

Chef Sharron has an extensive food background in the greater Seattle area for the last thirty years. She is a UW graduate and has taught cooking classes often developing her own unique recipes.

Peasant Sausage Soup

2 lbs Kielbasa or Italian sausage
   (cut into 1/2" slices)
2 cloves garlic (minced)
2 onions (chopped)
Two 1-lb cans diced tomatoes with juices
2 C canned kidney beans (rinsed and drained)
1-1/2 C dry red wine
10 to 15 C beef stock
1 tsp dried basil
1 tsp dried oregano
1 TBSP chopped parsley
1 medium green bell pepper
   (seeded and diced)
2 medium zucchini (sliced)
2 C uncooked pasta noodles
salt and pepper *(to taste)*
Parmesan cheese *(for garnish)*

In a heavy stockpot, cook sausage over medium heat until lightly browned. Remove sausage to a paper towel to drain. Drain all but 1 TBSP of sausage oil from stockpot. Add garlic and onions to oil in stockpot and sauté for 3 minutes. Add tomatoes, kidney beans, wine and 10 C beef stock, basil and oregano. Simmer uncovered, for 30 minutes.

Add parsley, green pepper, zucchini, noodles, salt and pepper and sausage. Simmer covered an additional 25 minutes. At this time, add more stock if soup is too thick.

Serve with Parmesan cheese on top.

Serves 10

RESTAURANT LE PICHET

Restaurant Le Pichet
1933 First Ave
Seattle, WA 98101

206-256-1499

Hours
Sun-Thurs 8am-midnight
Fri-Sat 8am-2am

© 2002 Bob Peterson

Le Pichet offers traditional and regional French specialties, a wide assortment of house-made charcuterie and more then 40 wines by the glass, pitcher (pichet) or bottle.

Proprietors Joanne Herron and Jim Drohman are both University of Washington Alumni.

Joanne received her BA in Communications in 1985.

Jim earned a BS in Aeronautics and Astronautics, in 1985 and a MS in Aeronautics and Astronautics in 1989.

Restaurant Le Pichet is open for lunch and dinner 7 days a week.

Gratin Lyonnais (Lyon-Style Onion Soup)

2-1/2 lbs yellow onions
4 cloves garlic
1/2 stick unsalted butter
1-1/2 C Sherry
3/4 C dry white wine
1 sprig thyme
1 bay leaf
2 quarts chicken stock
salt and black pepper
8 large croutons
2 C grated Gruyere

Peel the onions and slice thinly. Peel the garlic and slice thinly. Wash the thyme and chop finely. In a large soup pot over medium heat, sweat the onions and garlic with the butter, stirring often, until richly colored. Add the sherry. Increase the heat and cook until it is almost completely reduced. Add white wine and reduce by half. Add the thyme and bay leaf and enough chicken stock to give a nice ratio of stock to onions. Simmer to combine the flavors, about 20 minutes. Carefully skim off any fat. Correct the seasoning with salt and black pepper.

To make the croutons, bake 1/2-inch thick slices of hearty bread on a sheet pan in a 350-degree oven until dry and crisp.

Spoon the soup into individual bowls. Top first with a crouton and then a nice layer of grated Gruyere cheese. Heat under the broiler until crusty and golden. Serve immediately with a light red wine such as a Beaujolais or Cabernet Franc.

Serves 8

LOWELL-HUNT CATERING

Lowell-Hunt Catering
Private Facilities
1111 Fairview Ave N
Seattle 98109
206-264-0400
★
Lowell-Hunt Cafe
14810 NE 145th St
Woodinville 98072
425-486-4072
CAFE HOURS
Mon-Fri: Open at 8am
     for scones and coffee
Lunch: Mon-Sat 11am-2:30pm
Dinner: Tue-Thurs 5pm-8pm

www.lowell-hunt.com

In 1994 Russell Lowell and Jonathan Hunt joined forces and Lowell-Hunt Catering comenced. Now one of the most sought-after teams in Seattle, their primary goal is to continually surpass expectations with both their food and service.

Russell *(far left)* spent several years developing his culinary expertise working and managing the kitchens at a broad range of regionally and nationally-known restaurants. He spent 6 years as chef of Daniel's Broiler at Leschi where he first worked with Jonathan. Russell introduced discerning patrons to wild game specials and wild game cooking classes.

An instinctive love of great food led Russell to apprentice with master chefs while still in high school.

Wild Mushroom Soup

3 oz pancetta (diced)
1 TBSP peppercorns
2 TBSP olive oil
1/2 leek (white part only, diced)
1 yellow onion (diced)
6 cloves garlic (halved)
1 large carrot (diced)
1 stalk celery (diced)
1 lb mushrooms (sliced)
  (any variety[ies] you prefer)
16 C chicken broth *(fresh or canned)*
  (heated)

2 bay leaves
1 bunch fresh thyme
1/4 bunch parsley (stems only)
1 oz porcini mushrooms
  (dried, wrapped in cheesecloth)
salt *(to taste)*
fresh ground white pepper *(to taste)*
1/2 lb butter
1 oz Marsala wine
  (used for its walnutty taste)
1/2 lemon (fresh-squeezed juice)
fresh ravioli *(optional)*

In a large pot, sauté pancetta and peppercorns with 2 TBSP olive oil, until crispy.

Add leek, onion, garlic, carrot and celery. Sauté until translucent.

(continued on next page)

LOWELL-HUNT CATERING

Lowell-Hunt Catering
Private Facilities
1111 Fairview Ave N
Seattle 98109
206-264-0400
★
Lowell-Hunt Cafe
14810 NE 145th St
Woodinville 98072
425-486-4072
CAFE HOURS
Mon-Fri: Open at 8am
 for scones and coffee
Lunch: Mon-Sat 11am -2:30pm
Dinner: Tue-Thurs 5pm-8pm

www.lowell-hunt.com

Jonathan Hunt *(far left)* honed his culinary and leadership skills in the kitchens of several Seattle restaurants. A high-energy, self-taught chef, Jonathan strengthened his expertise through a keen interest in cookbooks and a passion for learning and experimenting with recipes.

As a perfectionist, he is committed to flawless execution and works tirelessly to create the perfect culinary experience for Lowell-Hunt guests.

Lowell-Hunt Catering employs over 30 full-time staff. Its headquarters are located on Lake Union in Seattle. The company also maintains a quaint dining facility behind the historic Hollywood Schoolhouse in Woodinville. This location provides additional opportunities to experience Lowell-Hunt's fine cuisine in a cafe-style setting.

Wild Mushroom Soup *continued*

In a separate pan, sauté mushrooms until almost dry and then add to the pot.

Add heated chicken broth, bay leaves, thyme, parsley stems and sachet of dried porcini (in the cheesecloth). Bring to a boil, then simmer until reduced by 1/2.

Strain through a chinois (metal mesh strainer) and season with salt and pepper.

Remove sachet of porcini. Discard cheesecloth. Dice porcinis and reserve.

Just prior to serving, using a blender (handheld, preferably), incorporate butter into hot broth.

Add white wine. Finish with lemon juice and diced porcini mushrooms.

Garnish with a few fresh ravioli. *(Optional)*

Makes 8 Cups

ROVER'S RESTAURANT

Rover's Restaurant
2808 Madison Ave
Seattle, WA 98112

206-325-7442

Dinner
Tue-Sat 5:30pm-8:30pm

Reservations recommended

All major cards accepted

www.rovers-seattle.com

Award-winning Chef Thierry Rautureau, beloved locally and respected nationally for his cuisine as well as his philanthropy, is celebrating his 15th year of ownership of the acclaimed Rover's Restaurant. This intimate restaurant, located in Seattle's Madison Valley, is nestled in a private courtyard and filled with art and sophistication—a trademark of the friendly "Chef in the Hat!!!" A James Beard winner for "Best Chef in the Pacific Northwest," Rautureau has been recognized for several years running in the Zagat Survey as having Seattle's top rated restaurant. He has received many more awards and honors as well. Come enjoy Thierry's innovative Northwest contemporary cuisine with a French accent.

Warm Alaskan Halibut Salad with Tomato Marinade

Tomato Marinade
2 medium tomatoes (diced small)
4 shallots (chopped)
2 garlic cloves (chopped)
1/3 C basil leaves (julienne-cut)
1/2 C aged Balsamic vinegar
1/4 C extra virgin olive oil
1/2 tsp ground black peppercorn

Combine all the ingredients in a bowl and refrigerate covered for at least one hour.

Salad
2 TBSP extra virgin olive oil
16 oz fresh halibut (cut in 4 oz slices)

Pour olive oil in a hot sauté pan and cook Halibut on each side for about 30 seconds. To serve, lay the halibut over the Tomato Marinade.

Serves 4

SEMIAHMOO RESORT

Semiahmoo Resort
9565 Semiahmoo Pkwy
Blaine, WA   98230

800-770-7992

www.semiahmoo.com

Nestled on a 1,100-acre wildlife preserve, Semiahmoo Resort is surrounded by water on three sides, offers an endless stretch of beach, views of the Canadian Gulf Islands and acres of wooded trails. Guests enjoy friendly, gracious service and sweeping views of snow-capped mountains, soaring eagles and a variety of outdoor activities. Close to the San Juan Islands and Cascade mountain range, Semiahmoo is just two hours north of Seattle and one hour south of Vancouver, and is a tranquil, yet activity-rich, destination.

"The cuisine at Semiahmoo is straight-forward and uncomplicated food with bright flavors focusing on seasonality and showcasing local farmers. The resort offers a wide selection of dining options including the creative flavors of Stars Restaurant."

- Bryan Weener, Executive Chef

Roasted Beets with Whole Grain Mustard, Orange and Sheep's Milk Cheese

2 lb Chioga, gold or red beets
  (or a mixture of all three)
3 TBSP olive oil
1 TBSP kosher salt
1/4 tsp pepper
2 handfuls arugula leaves
sheep's milk cheese *(like Pecorino or Locatelli)*

Preheat oven to 350 degrees. In a large bowl toss beets with oil, salt and pepper. Place on a tray and bake for 30 to 45 minutes *(depending on the size of the beets)*. The beets are done when you insert a toothpick into them and the beet gives little resistance. Let the beets cool slightly and peel with the help of a towel. Slice beets in half, then the halves into thirds.

Place beets in a large bowl with arugula leaves and dress with Dressing (just enough so that everything is lightly coated). Divide onto six salad plates and top with shaved sheep's milk cheese.

Dressing
2 C orange juice
2 oz champagne vinegar
1 TBSP minced ginger root
3 cloves garlic
1 C olive oil
2 TBSP whole grain mustard

In a small pot reduce everything (except olive oil and mustard) by 2/3 volume. After reduced, place in a blender. On high speed, add oil in a slow steady stream. Pour into a bowl and add mustard. Season with salt and pepper. **Makes 6 Salads**

SZMANIA'S RESTAURANT

SZMANIA'S in Magnolia
3321 W McGraw St
Seattle, WA 98199
206-284-7305

★

SZMANIA'S in Kirkland
148 Lake Street S
Kirkland, WA 98033
425-803-3310

Reservations recommended

www.szmanias.com

SZMANIA's *(pronounced "Smahn-ya's" the "z" is silent)* opened in 1990 as Magnolia Village's neighborhood bistro. Chef/owner Ludger Szmania (former Executive Chef of the Four Seasons Olympic Hotel) and his wife, Julie, actively operate the upscale bistro with its open kitchen, warm ambiance, fresh menu and skilled professional staff. The menu changes regularly featuring several "split" dinners for lighter appetites. The menu always reflects what's fresh and the chef's mood!

In May 2001, SZMANIA opened a second location in vibrant downtown Kirkland. It features a circular bar, exhibition kitchen, seating for 120, and offers outdoor patio dining in warm weather.

Lobster Mashed Potatoes

One 1-lb lobster
1/2 C carrots (1/2" slices)
1/2 C onion (1/2" slices)
1/2 C celery (1/2" slices)
1 bay leaf
2 TBSP olive oil
1 TBSP tomato paste

2 lbs Yukon gold potatoes (peeled)
1 TBSP butter
pinch of nutmeg
1/4 C heavy cream
1/3 C finely chopped chives
salt and pepper to taste

Boil lobster in lightly salted water for about 5-7 minutes. When cooked, put lobster into ice water to cool and reserve hot broth.

Cut lobster open from head to tail and remove all meat from claws and tail.

Heat a 4-quart pot on high heat. Add lobster body, shells, vegetables, bay leaf and olive oil. Cook everything over high heat for about 10 minutes. Add tomato paste and let caramelize to a dark brown. Add a touch of lobster broth to release the color from the bottom of the pot; do this over again about 4-5 times for maximum flavor.

(continued on next page)

SZMANIA'S RESTAURANT

SZMANIA'S in Magnolia
3321 W McGraw St
Seattle, WA 98199
206-284-7305

★

SZMANIA'S in Kirkland
148 Lake Street S
Kirkland, WA 98033
425-803-3310

Reservations recommended

www.szmanias.com

SZMANIA's is "one of the happiest and classiest dining rooms in Seattle," wrote John Hinterberger of The Seattle Times.

The News Tribune awarded SZMANIA'S in Kirkland as its #1-TOP choice for dining (2001). It continues to receive culinary accolades with its contemporary Northwest regional menu melded with American favorites and German specialties.

Both SZMANIA'S offer a full bar as well as an extensive wine list that focuses on excellent regional selections. A private dining room, with fireplace, seats up to 30 guests with custom menus for every party. A children's menu is always available.

Lobster Mashed Potatoes *continued*

Cover the lobster and vegetables with more lobster broth and let remain for about 30-40 minutes; then strain.

Boil peeled potatoes in lightly salted water until done, about 30 minutes. Put them through a ricer into a bowl. Add butter, about 1/3 cup of lobster stock and cream. Salt and pepper to taste.

Cut the lobster meat into cubes (keep the claws for garnish). Add meat and chives to the potatoes. (Additional cream may be added to taste.)

Garnish with lobster claws and serve.

Serves 4

RESTAURANT ZOË

Restaurant Zoë
2137 Second Ave
Seattle, WA 98121
(in Belltown, on the corner of Second & Blanchard)

206-256-2060

Dinner
Mon-Sat 5pm-10pm

MC, Visa and AmEx

www.restaurantzoe.com

Owners, Scott and Heather Staples opened the doors of Restaurant Zoë to the public in September 2000.

Named after their toddler daughter, Restaurant Zoë is located in Seattle's eclectic Belltown neighborhood where Chef Staples is committed to offering an innovative, produce-driven menu in a contemporary, yet comfortable, bistro setting.

Seattle Magazine says Scott and Heather Staples "…have created one of the city's freshest restaurants smack dab in the middle of Belltown. High windows make the passing crowds part of the scene and the menu makes the most of regional, seasonal foods."

Grilled Romaine Salad with Apples, Smoked Bacon and Roquefort Dressing

4 thick slices smoked bacon
   (cut into strips)
1 head romaine lettuce
2 TBSP olive oil
pepper

kosher salt
1 crisp, sweet apple (peeled, quartered
   and thinly sliced)
1/2 C (about 4 oz) crumbled Roquefort
   cheese

Fry bacon until crisp and then drain on paper towels.

Preheat the grill to a very high heat.

Remove the outer leaves from the lettuce and trim off the top 2 to 3 inches. Cut the lettuce in half lengthwise. Brush the lettuce with olive oil on all sides and season with salt and pepper.

Place the lettuce cut side down on the grill until good grill marks appear, about 2 to 3 minutes. Flip the lettuce and grill the other side until the romaine is lightly caramelized

(continued on next page)

RESTAURANT ZOË

Restaurant Zoë
2137 Second Ave
Seattle, WA 98121
(in Belltown, on the
corner of Second &
Blanchard)

206-256-2060

Dinner
Mon-Sat 5pm-10pm

MC, Visa and AmEx

www.restaurantzoe.com

z o ë
R E S T A U R A N T

Seattle Weekly wrote: "...the space is classy but not flashy, the service is helpful, but not obtrusive, and the clientele is mixed in age, style and clique. The food, like that at fine French bistros, combines the classic with the intriguing."

Alaska Airlines In-Flight Magazine said, "Restaurant Zoë is an urban restaurant whose corner space invited us in with floor-to-ceiling windows showing a bustling dining room and a lively downtown bar.

"The rest of the restaurant made us feel relaxed with it's subdued hues of rose, faded denim blue and artichoke green."

Grilled Romaine Salad with Apples, Smoked Bacon and Roquefort Dressing *continued*

and warmed through, but still crisp in the center, about 1 minute.

Remove the stems from the lettuce and arrange each half on a plate. Scatter with bacon, apples, and cheese. Drizzle about 1/4 cup dressing over each plate. Serve immediately.

Roquefort Dressing

6 oz (about 3/4 C) crumbled Roquefort cheese
6 TBSP red wine vinegar
1/4 C peeled sliced shallots
3/4 C olive oil
1/4 tsp kosher salt
1/4 tsp pepper

Combine cheese, vinegar and shallots in the bowl of a food processor and blend until smooth. Gradually add the olive oil, salt and pepper. Makes about 1-1/2 cups. (Keep unused portion refrigerated.)

Serves 2

WASHINGTON STARS

Entrées

ASSAGGIO

Assaggio Ristorante
2010 Fourth Ave
Seattle, WA 98121

206-441-1399

Dinner
Mon-Sat 5pm-10pm

Closed Sundays and Holidays

www.assaggioseattle.com

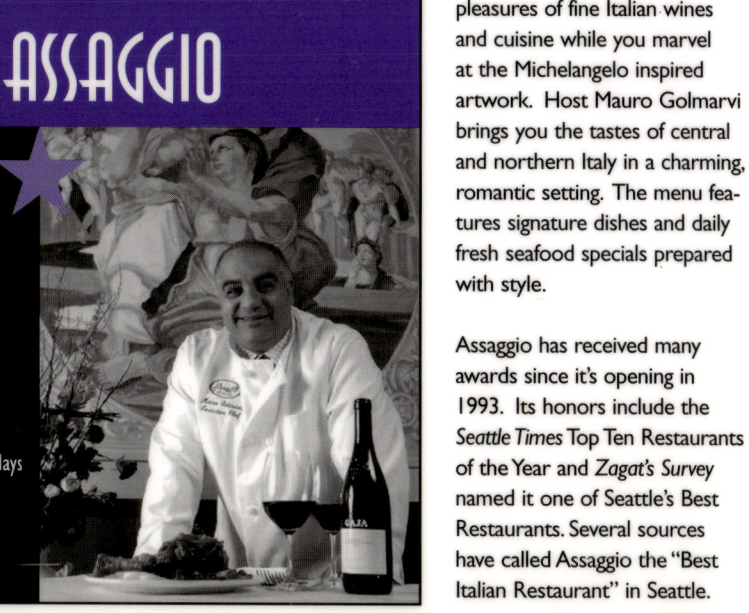

At Assaggio you can pamper your soul with the sensual pleasures of fine Italian wines and cuisine while you marvel at the Michelangelo inspired artwork. Host Mauro Golmarvi brings you the tastes of central and northern Italy in a charming, romantic setting. The menu features signature dishes and daily fresh seafood specials prepared with style.

Assaggio has received many awards since it's opening in 1993. Its honors include the *Seattle Times* Top Ten Restaurants of the Year and *Zagat's* Survey named it one of Seattle's Best Restaurants. Several sources have called Assaggio the "Best Italian Restaurant" in Seattle.

Cappelletti alla Mauro

- 1 lb giant tortellini
- 2 lbs fresh prawns
- 2 TBSP olive oil
- 1/2 C dry white wine
- 1 pint heavy whipping cream
- 1 eggplant (cubed)
- 1 TBSP garlic (chopped)
- 5 oz marinara sauce
- 1 oz basil (chopped)
- 1 oz Italian parsley (finely chopped)
- salt and pepper to taste

In a pot of boiling water, with a dash of salt, cook pasta 5 minutes while preparing sauce. In a sauté pan, sauté garlic and eggplant in olive oil until garlic is golden.

Add marinara sauce and wine. Bring to boil. Add prawns and cream, stir and reduce to simmer. Drain pasta and add to sauce with basil.

Stir and serve. Garnish with parsley.

Serves 4

BARKING FROG

Barking Frog
Located at Willows Lodge
14580 NE 145th Street
Woodinville, WA 98072

Restaurant: 425-424-2999
Lodge: 425-424-3900

Brunch
Sat-Sun 10:00am-2:30pm

Lunch
Mon-Fri 11:00am-2:30pm

Dinner
Mon-Sun 5:00pm-10:00pm

www.barkingfrog.org
www.willowslodge.com

Barking Frog is a casual bistro featuring country fresh Northwest Cuisine and an extensive Northwest wine collection. It is located at the picturesque Willows Lodge in Woodinville, Washington.

Willows Lodge is known as a Northwest celebration of the senses. In keeping with the theme of the lodge, the restaurant has embraced the traditions and lifestyles of the Native American culture.

"They have taught us that when a frog is in a good, healthy environment, you will hear "bark-ing." This is a sign of peace and harmony. We chose our name because we think the Barking Frog is the perfect place for you to experience this." – *Tom Black*

Seared Ahi Tuna with Potato Rosti, Soy Emulsion and Chives

Four 2.5-3 oz Ahi tuna portions

Chives (chopped) *(for garnish)*

Season Ahi with salt and white pepper. Lightly sear rare to medium-rare. Slice thinly and place across Potato Rosti *(recipe follows)*. Pour Soy Emulsion Sauce *(recipe follows)* around Ahi and sprinkle chives on top.

Potato Rosti
2 Yukon Gold potatoes
   (shredded with mandoline)
1/2 bunch parsley
   (washed and finely chopped)

salt
white pepper
duck fat* (or Canola oil) *(for cooking)*

Combine potatoes, parsley, salt and pepper. Heat duck fat in a 6-inch or 8-inch non-stick frying pan over medium heat. Add potato mixture. Cook without stirring for about 10 minutes. Gently press down on the potatoes to compact them.

Flip the pancake and cook until golden on the second side, another 5 to 7 minutes. Add more duck fat to the pan if necessary. Salt and pepper to taste.

(continued on next page)   *see Appendix

BARKING FROG

Barking Frog
Located at Willows Lodge
14580 NE 145th Street
Woodinville, WA 98072

Restaurant: 425-424-2999
Lodge: 425-424-3900

Brunch
Sat-Sun 10:00am-2:30pm

Lunch
Mon-Fri 11:00am-2:30pm

Dinner
Mon-Sun 5:00pm-10:00pm

www.barkingfrog.org
www.willowslodge.com

Tom Black was named Executive Chef and General Manager of Barking Frog in September of 2001. Tom began his culinary career at age 15 working in a family-operated restaurant in Indiana. He left Indiana to serve three years in the U.S. Army's 82nd Airborne Division at Fort Bragg, NC. Black then returned to Indiana to prepare for enrollment at the New England Culinary Institute where he earned his degree in 1995.

Tom has worked at the Sheraton Seattle and Fullers Restaurant before coming to Barking Frog. His menus reflect his focus on regionally-influenced, globally-inspired cuisine and in 2001 and 2002, the prestigious Zagat awarded him with Best Northwest Cuisine.

Seared Ahi Tuna with Potato Rosti, Soy Emulsion and Chives *continued*

Soy Emulsion Sauce

1-1/2 C soy sauce
1-1/2 C white wine
1-1/2 TBSP honey
1/2 TBSP black pepper
1-1/2 bay leaves

5 garlic cloves (crushed)
1 stalks lemon grass* (crushed)
3/4-inch piece ginger (sliced)
3/4 lb cold butter (cubed)
chives (chopped) *(as garnish)*

Combine all ingredients except butter. Bring to a simmer. Reduce by half. Let cool. (May be stored in the refrigerator for up to 2 weeks.)

When ready to serve, heat sauce and whip in butter. Drizzle sauce around Ahi and potatoes. Top with chives.

Serves 4   *see Appendix*

¡CACTUS!

4220 E Madison
Madison Park
Seattle, WA 98112
206-324-4140

★

121 Park Lane
Kirkland, WA
425-893-9799

Lunch
Mon-Sat 11:30am-3pm
Dinner
Mon-Thurs 5pm-10pm
Fri-Sat 5pm-11pm
Sun 4pm-10pm
www.cactusrestaurant.com

Cactus! features the flavors of Mexico and the Southwest. Executive Chef Maritza Texeria's love for creating wonderful food is best told in her own words:

"As a little girl, I would hang out in my mom's kitchen and beg to peel carrots or snap peas, something that I could do in the kitchen instead of going out to play! As I look back now, the strange look on my mother's face at my request suddenly makes sense. I guess I've always been drawn to cooking, even when it has meant doing prep work. Though prep seems to be a never-ending task (and it is in a restaurant), it is well worth it when you have a savory dish like this one to share with friends and family."

Conchita Pibil

This recipe is great to make for a party. Serve with warm corn tortillas, onions and sour cream.

1 achiote spice bar (annatto seed paste)*	6 lb pork shoulder/butt (bone-in)
1 C water (boiling)	*(call ahead to order from butcher or meat department)*
16 oz orange juice concentrate	
1 C water	2 limes (split in half) (4 halves total)
1/4 C corn oil	1/2 C cumin (ground)
1/2 C rice vinegar	5 bay leaves
	2 TBSP kosher salt

Place achiote spice bar in a mixing bowl and pour 1 cup boiling water over it. Gently whisk until the achiote bar is completely dissolved. Set aside.

In a separate mixing bowl, combine orange juice concentrate and 1 cup water. Whisk until orange juice concentrate is fully dissolved. Set aside.

Preheat oven to 400 degrees.

(continued on next page)   *see Appendix

Conchita Pibil *continued*

Place an 8-quart (or larger) braising pot on the stove (empty) and turn on heat to high. Let the braising pot get hot, about 4 minutes.

Very carefully, pour the corn oil into the pot and then place the pork shoulder/butt in the pot. Let sit untouched for 2 minutes, lightly browning the meat, then turn and repeat until all sides are lightly browned.

Take out the pork and set aside. Remove the excess oil from the pan.

Deglaze the pot with 1/4 cup rice vinegar. Add in achiote spice mixture, orange juice mixture and remaining ingredients (1/4 cup rice vinegar, lime halves, cumin, bay leaves and salt). Stir with a wooden spoon, mixing all ingredients.

Bring to a boil. Turn off heat and add in the pork.

(continued below)

Cover pot with an oven-safe lid or aluminum foil. Place in the oven and bake for 2-1/2 hours, turning over once halfway through the cooking process.

Carefully remove the lid. Place a china cap or large strainer over a food-safe container. Strain out all of the liquid and reserve. Take out the pork bone and the lime halves and discard.

Place the pork back in the braising pot and using two forks, shred all of the meat. Return the liquid to the braising pot and mix well.

Use immediately or cool down and refrigerate.

Serves 6 to 8

THE CAPTAIN WHIDBEY INN

The Captain Whidbey Inn
2072 W Capt Whidbey Inn Rd
Coupeville, WA 98239

360-678-4097
1-800-366-4097

Owned by Captain John Colby Stone

Activities include golf, sea-kyaking,
horseback riding, and sailing on
Capt. Stone's 52' ketch "Cutty Sark."

Checks and All Major Credit Cards

www.captainwhidbey.com

The
Captain Whidbey
Inn

The Captain Whidbey Inn has been offering outstanding lodging, food and drink from the wooded shore of Penn Cove since 1907. Quaint rooms in the historic main building and luxurious cabins and cottages feature featherbeds and warm down comforters.

The Inn's dining room features an exquisite view of Penn Cove in a warm, rustic setting. The fare is classic country inn with a Northwest flavor. Abundant fresh seafoods, world famous Penn Cove mussels, fresh herbs and vegetables from private gardens all contribute to an excellent regional reputation.

Steven Clarke stands 6' 7" in his tiny kitchen. He worked in Alaska as a Commercial Fisherman to pay for his education in the Culinary Arts prior to coming to The Inn as Chef.

Captain Whidbey's Penn Cove Ginger Mussels

- 4 TBSP fresh ginger root (finely chopped)
- 2 TBSP diced scallions *(can substitute Chinese garlic chives)*
- 2 TBSP fresh garlic (finely chopped)
- 2 tsp black pepper
- 1 Chipolte pepper *(from a 6 oz can)*
- 1 C rice vinegar
- 1/4 C soy sauce
- 2 C sake
- 1 lb uncooked mussels

Finely chop all vegetables. (If using a food processor, add a little of the vinegar and soy sauce while processing.)

Put all chopped vegetables and their juices in a large cooking pot. Add remaining vinegar and soy sauce. Mix in sake. Add 1 lb uncooked mussels and cover with lid. Heat and cook mussels for approximately 12 minutes. They are ready to eat when the shells open.

Serve immediately.

(The sauce may be made up to a week in advance prior to adding the mussels and cooking.)

Serves 4

CHATEAU STE. MICHELLE

Chateau Ste. Michelle
Vineyards & Wineries
14111 NE 145th St
Woodinville, WA 98072
425-488-1133

John Sarich conducts cooking classes, wine and food tastings, wine dinners and special events.

Call for more information or check out his website www.bestoftaste.com

Few chefs enjoy access to a greater bounty of world-class wines and fresh foods than Chateau Ste. Michelle's Culinary Director, John Sarich. "It's incredibly exciting to live in the Pacific Northwest", says John. "Not only do we have an outstanding variety of ingredients from the land and sea, we also have exceptional wines from Washington's Columbia Valley, where long summer days and crisp autumn nights produce ideal conditions for well balanced wines."

John's innovative approach to matching food and wine reflects his unique culinary background. His wine and food pairings have delighted discriminating palates across the country.

Argentinean Style Mixed Grill

Typically an Argentinean grill has a combination of meat, fowl and organ meats. You can mix and match different cuts of meat to your liking.

1/2 lb flank steak or strip steak
1 small (1 lb or less) pork tenderloin
2 young chickens, quail or game hens (cut in half)
1/4 C Columbia Crest Cabernet Sauvignon
lemon wedges *(as garnish)*

Scoop some of the Marinade/Salsa *(recipe on next page)* over the meats and rub gently. Sprinkle the meat and fowl with the Cabernet and toss together. Let marinate at least 1 hour or overnight.

Grill the chickens first, until done. Then grill the meat to medium-rare. Slice and place on a platter and scoop more of the Marinade/Salsa over the meats.

Serve with lemon wedges, tossed green salad and good crusty French bread.

Wine Recommendations: Columbia Crest Grand Estate Cabernet Sauvignon or Chateau Ste. Michelle Syrah.

(continued on next page)

CHATEAU STE. MICHELLE

Chateau Ste. Michelle
    Vineyards & Wineries
14111 NE 145th St
Woodinville, WA 98072
425-488-1133

For a full listing of all
the events at the winery,
go to their website

www.chateau-ste-michelle.com

Chateau Ste Michelle

VINEYARDS & WINERIES

Chateau Ste. Michelle is Washington State's oldest and most prestigious winery.

Tradition, innovation and the highest standards are the essence of Chateau Ste. Michelle. They grow their own grapes and use the finest French oak barrels. Their winemakers have worked and trained in Europe and their wines are always included among the "Top Wines of the World."

Their *Vintage Reserve Club* and winery tours and tastings will help you learn more about this venerable passion.

Chateau Ste. Michelle also hosts several open-air concerts each year featuring world-renowned musicians.

Argentinean Style Mixed Grill *continued*

Marinade/Salsa

- 1 yellow onion (diced small)
- 1 red pepper (diced small)
- 4 cloves garlic (diced small)
- 1 C Italian parsley (finely chopped)
- pinch pepper flakes
- 1/4 tsp salt
- 2 TBSP sweetened rice wine vinegar
- 1 TBSP lemon juice
- 1/2 C (more or less) extra virgin olive oil

Mix all the ingredients (*except olive oil*) in a medium-size bowl.

Add the olive oil a little at a time until you have the consistency of loose pesto.

Serves 4

CHUCKANUT MANOR

Chuckanut Manor
Restaurant and B&B
3056 Chuckanut Dr
Bow, WA 98232
360-766-6191

Sunday Brunch 10:30am
Lunch Tue-Sat 11:30am
Dinner Tue-Thurs & Sat 3pm
Friday Seafood Smorgy 5pm

Closed Mondays

All major credit cards

www.chuckanutmanor.com

The "Manor" has been serving the Northwest for over 35 years. Under the direction of Pat Woolcock, a 1970 UW graduate, and Chef Margarito Brito, the "Manor" provides a variety of dining experiences in a setting that overlooks Samish Bay and the San Juan Islands. The Friday Smorgy is outstanding and the Brunch is award-winning. Stay over at the Bed and Breakfast for a full "Manor" experience.

For more information, their menu, etc... check out their website.

Directions:

Located south of Bellingham
Northbound on I-5, from Seattle:
Exit 231
(Chuckanut Dr./Bow-Edison)
The drive is well worth it!

Chuckanut Manor Crab Au Gratin

sea salt and/or pickling spice
2 C heavy cream
1 tsp garlic (1 clove finely minced)
1/2 tsp lemon juice
2 oz chopped spinach

3 oz crabmeat
3 oz cocktail shrimp
salt and pepper (to taste)
1/4 C Parmesan cheese
One 2-lb Dungeness crab

Cook crab in boiling water seasoned with sea salt or pickling spice or both. Cut legs off and hollow out shell. Shake the crabmeat from the body and set aside. Save shell.

Combine cream, garlic and lemon juice in a saucepan over medium heat and reduce by half. Add spinach, crabmeat and shrimp. Salt and pepper to taste. Put mixture in crab shell and top with Parmesan cheese. Bake in oven at 375 degrees until brown. Warm legs and arrange around shell. Serve with warm butter or mayonnaise if desired. *(Who knows—maybe a little Tabasco, too!)*

Serves 6 to 8

COHO CAFE

Coho Cafe
8976 161st Ave NE
Redmond, WA 98052
425-885-2646

★

6130 E Lk Sammamish Pkwy
Issaquah, WA 98029
425-391-4040

Open 7 days a week
Lunch 11am-4pm
Dinner 4pm
Sunday Brunch 10am

www.cohocafe.com

The Coho Cafe is spontaneous, stylish and energetic. It is a gathering place for any occasion featuring wok cooking and fruit-wood smoking. Dine on distinctive seafood and many more exciting and affordable dishes. Expect a warm and comfortable environment with genuine service.

Chef Chris Hill brings his eclectic syle and diverse background to the Coho Cafe menu. With Latin and Pacific Rim influences, he creates bold flavors with distinctive, high-quality ingredients and an emphasis on fresh seafood. A graduate of the Culinary Insititute of America, Chris demonstrates his depth of experience and originality throughout the menu. We invite you to explore all that the Coho Cafe has to offer.

Applewood Smoked Salmon

Six (7 oz cuts) salmon fillets (skin off) 2 C applewood chips
12 TBSP salmon rub *(recipe follows)*

Rub both sides of the fillets with the salmon rub and let stand for about 20 minutes. Rinse off the rub and pat dry.

Using a smoker, start the chips burning. Once the chips are at a good flame, blow out the flame to create the smoke. Quickly place the fillets on the rack and close the lid so you lose minimal smoke. Smoke for 20 minutes.

Remove salmon and refrigerate.

At this point, the fillets can be pan-seared, grilled or oven-baked.

Salmon Rub
1/2 C chili powder
1/2 C granulated onion
1-1/2 C kosher salt
1/2 C ground mixed peppercorn blend
(white, green, black and pink)
1/4 C cinnamon (ground)
1/4 C nutmeg (ground)

Serves 6

HUNT CLUB

Hunt Club
In the Sorrento Hotel
900 Madison Street
Seattle, WA 98104

Phone: 206-343-6156

Breakfast Daily 7am-10am
Brunch Sat-Sun 10am-2:30pm
Lunch Mon-Fri 11am-2:30pm
Dinner Daily 6pm-10pm
Pre-Fixe Dinner
Sun-Thurs 5pm-6pm & 9pm-10pm

www.hotelsorrento.com

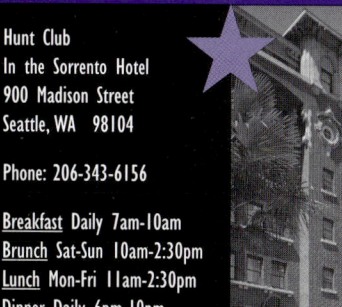

The Hunt Club at the Sorrento Hotel showcases the bounty of the Northwest in every meal with ingredients chosen from among the finest in-season local and artisan-farmed products, including organic products whenever available.

In 1909, the Sorrento opened its doors to coincide with the Alaska Yukon Exposition. Pioneer clothing merchant, Samuel Rosenberg, owned the hotel which he named after his favorite city in Italy.

Later, during hard times, he traded the hotel for Bear Creek Orchards near Medford, OR. The exchange was once characterized as "trading a lemon for a pear," as his sons, Harry and David turned the orchards into a multi-million dollar business.

Alaskan Halibut with Tagliatelle of Vegetables, Beurre Blanc and American Caviar

Four (6 oz each) Alaskan halibut fillets
salt and pepper (to taste)
Tagliatelle of Vegetables *(recipe next page)*
Beurre Blanc *(recipe next page)*

American caviars (white sturgeon,
  whitefish and salmon)* *(for garnish)*
fresh chervil* *(for garnish)*

Season halibut with salt and pepper. Pan-sear until golden brown. Turn fillets. Place in baking dish and finish in a 350-degree oven until firm to touch (approximately 8 to 10 minutes).

Blanch tagliatelle of vegetables *al dente* (firm to the bite) and lightly sauté with butter. Place vegetables in the center of the plate with halibut on top. Lightly sauce with Beurre Blanc.

Garnish with caviar and fresh chervil.

(continued on next page)   *see Appendix

HUNT CLUB

Hunt Club
In the Sorrento Hotel
900 Madison Street
Seattle, WA 98104

Phone: 206-343-6156

Breakfast Daily 7am-10am
Brunch Sat-Sun 10am-2:30pm
Lunch Mon-Fri 11am-2:30pm
Dinner Daily 6pm-10pm
Pre-Fixe Dinner
Sun-Thurs 5pm-6pm
& 9pm-10pm

www.hotelsorrento.com

Hunt Club Executive Chef Brian Scheehser is passionate about his work. He heads a staff of 13 and oversees breakfast, lunch and dinner. His latest menu is heavily influenced by culinary trends from both the Northwest and Mediterranean regions. This fusion was inspired by the Hotel itself—a Northwest institution with its architectural roots firmly fixed in the Mediterranean heritage of its namesake city.

Scheehser's food combinations are innovative, but his training is very traditional. As a student at the Culinary Institute of America in Hyde Park, New York, he specialized in "garde mange" (the preparation of cold stew, soups, salads and patés terrines).

In his spare time, he tends his acre garden and four beehives, producing 25 gallons of some of Seattle's finest honey.

Alaskan Halibut with Tagliatelle of Vegetables, Beurre Blanc and American Caviar *continued*

Tagliatelle of Vegetables

2 zucchini
2 yellow squash
1 carrot
1 leek (white part only)

Using a mandoline or knife, cut vegetables into long julienne strips, resembling tagliatelle pasta. For squash, only use the outer flesh and not the seeds.

Beurre Blanc

1 shallot (finely chopped)
2 oz white wine
1 oz lemon juice
1 oz heavy cream
8 oz butter
salt and pepper to taste

Combine the chopped shallot and the white wine. Sauté *au sec* (until dry). Add heavy cream and reduce slightly. Cut butter into 1-inch cubes and whisk slowly into the reduction until incorporated. Adjust the seasoning. If the sauce seems too flat, add a little more lemon juice. If the sauce seems too acidic, add a little more butter.

Serves 4

THE KINGFISH CAFE

The Kingfish Cafe
602 19th Ave E
Seattle, WA 98112
206-320-8757

Sunday Brunch
11am-2pm

Lunch
Mon, Wed, Thurs, Fri: 11:30am-2pm

Dinner
Mon, Wed, Thurs 6pm-9pm
Fri & Sat 6pm-10pm
Closed on Tuesdays

Cash or Checks only

The Kingfish Cafe is a wonderful place to meet friends for a drink and people-watch. This soulful, family-run restaurant is a must. It has won awards for Best Comfort Food as well as Best Dessert. The cafe serves up-scale soul food that's well worth the wait. The atmosphere is cozy and the wait staff are friendly and courteous. The vintage family photos hanging on the walls are a tribute to hard work and success.

Get there early for seating. They do not take reservations, but you won't be sorry you waited when you taste the great Fried Chicken Salad, Corn Muffins, Catfish, Crabcakes, etc...not to mention the desserts—they're huge!

Macaroni and Cheese

2-1/2 C elbow pasta (uncooked)
1/2 gallon boiling water
dash of olive oil
1 C white onion (diced)
1 C green pepper (diced)
1/4 C butter-flavored liquid oil
1 TBSP salt
1 TBSP pepper

One (12-1/2 oz) can cream of mushroom soup
3 eggs
1/4 C milk (2%)
2 C heavy cream
10 oz cheddar cheese (shredded)
10 oz pepperjack cheese (shredded)

Preheat oven to 350 degrees. Cook elbow pasta in boiling water until al dente. Strain and put in a large bowl with a dash of olive oil. Toss and set aside.

Sauté onion and green pepper in butter-oil until translucent. Add salt and pepper. Add to pasta. Mix in cream of mushroom soup. In another bowl, mix eggs, milk and cream. Add to pasta mixture. Add half of cheese to pasta mixture. Mix well.

Grease a deep casserole dish and pour mixture in. Top with remaining cheese and cover with lightly oiled foil. Bake for one hour. Macaroni is done when center is set and top is lightly brown. Remove foil to cool. Let stand five minutes before serving.

Serves 4

RISTORANTE PARADISO

Ristorante Paradiso
120 Park Lane
Kirkland, WA 98033

425-889-8601

<u>Lunch</u>
Mon-Fri 11am-3pm
<u>Dinner</u>
Nightly 3pm-10:30pm

Major Credit Cards Accepted

www.ristoranteparadiso.com

Risorante Paradiso is owned by two brothers from Sardinia, Italy. Chef Fabrizio *(pictured left)* and Francesco Loi opened this jewel in 1991.

Even though Paradiso is a small restaurant on a small one-way street, everyone seems to know exactly where it is.

It is a genuine Italian ristorante serving authentic Italian favorites that are hard to find these days.

The cannelloni recipe included here is a special request from our editor, who travels regularly to Paradiso to enjoy this dish.

The service is attentive, but not overbearing as they create the feeling of dining in a small family-owned cafe in Sardinia.

Cannelloni di Fabrizio

1-1/2 to 2 lb veal top round roast* (boneless)
sage
olive oil *(for pan searing)*
3-4 carrots
3-4 stalks celery
1/2 lb Mortadella* *(smoked Italian sausage)*
1/2 C Parmesan cheese
1 egg (beaten)

6-8 oz Mozzarella cheese *(for stuffing crepes)*
16 crepes *(recipe on page 109)*
3 C Béchamel (white) sauce
   (recipe follows)
3 C tomato sauce *(recipe follows)*
2 C Parmesan cheese *(for topping crepes)*
8 oz Mozzarella cheese *(for topping crepes)*
Parmigiano Reggiano cheese *(Parmesan may be substituted)* *(freshly grated)*

The day before: *Make crepe batter and refrigerate at least 1 hour (but not more than 24 hours) before cooking crepes. (Tomato sauce may also be made a day ahead.)*

Preheat oven to 400 degrees. Cut roast in half and roll in sage for flavor. Coat the bottom of a roasting pan with olive oil. Heat on stove. When hot, add veal, carrots and celery. Pan sear the meat until golden brown. Transfer roasting pan with its ingredients to the oven.

Roast veal in oven for 20 minutes. Put veal through food processor twice using a medium shredding disc. Grind vegetables, Mortadella, 1/2 C Parmesan and 6-8 oz Mozzarella. Put meat, vegetables, Mortadella, Parmesan and Mozzarella through processor again. Add beaten egg. Set aside.

(continued on next page)   **see Appendix*

RISTORANTE PARADISO

Ristorante Paradiso
120 Park Lane
Kirkland, WA 98033

425-889-8601

Lunch
Mon-Fri 11am-3pm
Dinner
Nightly 3pm-10:30pm

Major Credit Cards Accepted

www.ristoranteparadiso.com

Chef/owner Fabrizio Loi is from the village of Triei on the island of Sardinia, Italy. In 1978, Fabrizio was accepted to Italy's national culinary college, the Instituto Professionale Alberghiero, where he completed an intensive three-year certificate program in all aspects of restaurant management and operations, graduating with honors in 1980.

Here in America he has created his special versions of traditional Italian recipes for your dining pleasure.

Risorante Paradiso has a wonderful quaint setting with an artist touch of chef Fabrizio's finest gourmet delights.

Cannelloni di Fabrizio *continued*

Cook crepes. Spoon approx. 1/3 C meat and vegetable mixture into center of cooked crepes.

Roll them up and place them side-by-side in a shallow, buttered casserole dish, cover with tomato sauce, Béchamel Sauce *(recipe below)*. Top with 2 C Parmesan and 8 oz shredded Mozzarella cheese. (Or, place two crepes in individual cannelloni dishes. Cover each dish with 1/3 C tomato sauce and 1/3 C Béchamel Sauce. Top with approximately 1/4 C Parmesan and 1 oz shredded Mozzarella cheese.)

Bake at 350 degrees until sauce bubbles and cheese turns golden brown. Serve immediately. Freshly grate pure Parmigiano Reggiano cheese over the top as a final touch. *(Parmesan cheese can be substituted.)*

Béchamel Sauce

6 TBSP butter	1 TBSP grated nutmeg
4 to 5 TBSP flour	3 C whole milk

Melt butter over low heat. Slowly stir in the flour and nutmeg and blend over low heat for 5 minutes. In a separate pan, gently heat milk. Remove from heat just as it begins to boil. Let milk cool slightly. Slowly add it to the "roux" (flour. butter and nutmeg paste). Over low heat, stir with a whisk or wooden spoon until sauce is thickened and smooth.

Makes 3 cups sauce

(continued on next page)

Cannelloni di Fabrizio *continued*

Crepes

4 eggs
1/4 tsp salt
2 C flour

2-1/4 C milk
1/4 butter (melted)

In medium bowl, combine eggs and salt. Alternating flour and milk, add slowly to the egg mixture while beating with a whisk. Beat in melted butter. Refrigerate for at least 1 hour, but not more than 24 hours.

Heat a crepe pan over medium-high heat. Add a few tablespoons batter to pan while holding it off the heat and quickly rotating it to spread the batter evenly. Return to heat and cook until golden brown. Turn and brown the other side for only a few seconds (until the liquid is firm).

Stack finished crepes on plate or waxed paper.

Crepes can be stored in the refrigerator for up 2 to 3 days. They will keep in the freezer up to 4 months, and should be separated with waxed paper and sealed in a freezer bag. **Makes 16 to 18 crepes.**

Cannelloni da Fabrizio *continued*

Tomato Sauce

1/4 C olive oil
2-3 cloves garlic (minced)
1-1/2 C onions (sliced)
One 28 oz can peeled tomatoes
1 tsp salt
1/2 tsp black pepper (freshly ground)
1/2 tsp basil

Heat oil and brown garlic in saucepan. Add onions and sauté approximately 10 minutes. Add tomatoes, salt, pepper and basil. Cover and cook over low heat about 1-1/2 hours. Purée mixture in a blender or put through a strainer.

Mixture may be stored overnight in a covered, non-metallic container.

Makes 3 cups sauce

Serves 6 to 8

PASTA & CO

Pasta & Co.

Bellevue
425-453-8760

Issaquah
425-391-2797

Redmond
425-881-1992

Queen Anne
206-283-1182

University Village
206-523-8594

www.pastaco.com

Pasta & Co. is Seattle's premiere retailer of high quality take-out foods and specialty groceries.

The 21-year-old company now has five stores, but its flagship is a quick walk from the UW campus in the west end of U Village.

Pasta & Co. stores offer a full menu of take-out foods from appetizers to entrees to desserts, both ready-to-eat and ready-to-bake. The ever changing selection keeps alive the thrill of discovery even in everyday food shopping.

Visit the Pasta & Co. website where you can learn daily what the store kitchens are cooking for your take-out dinner. Be sure to check out the stylishly fun items that go with them.

Chicken Baked in
Pasta & Co. Roasted Tomato Chutney Sauce

4 whole boneless chicken breasts
2 TBSP olive oil

One 12-oz jar *Pasta & Co. Roasted Tomato Chutney Sauce*

Lay 4 whole boneless chicken breasts in a single layer in oven-proof baking dish.

Pour the jar of *Pasta & Co. Roasted Tomato Chutney Sauce* and the olive oil over chicken. Cover tightly with foil.

Bake in preheated 375-degree oven for 40 minutes or until chicken is done.

Serve chicken and juices over a bed of couscous or rice.

Accompany with seasonal vegetables.

Serves 4 to 8

SALISH LODGE & SPA

Salish Lodge & Spa
6501 Railroad Ave SE
Snoqualmie, WA 98065

1-800-2-SALISH
1-800-272-5474
425-888-2556

MAIN DINING ROOM
Breakfast
Mon-Fri 7am-11am
Sat-Sun 7am-2pm
Dinner
Mon-Sun 5pm-10pm

ATTIC CAFÉ
11am-11pm

www.salishlodge.com

Each of the 91 guest rooms at Salish Lodge & Spa features a bedside wood-burning fireplace, two-person whirlpool tub, goosedown comforter, and a balcony or window seat.

The resort offers a variety of recreational activities, treatments at the award-winning Spa, contemporary Northwest cuisine, and personalized service.

For the eighth annual Gold List, 29,000 subscribers to *Condé Nast Traveler* participated in its annual Readers' Poll and have chosen the best of the best in travel. In their January 2002 issue, Salish Lodge & Spa was named one of the world's best resorts in five categories: rooms, service, restaurants, location and activities.

Mint and Nut Crusted Rack of Lamb with Russian Banana Fingerling Potato Purée

For that special occasion, Chef Mike Davis' rack of lamb will receive "oohs" and "aahs" from everyone at the dining room table.

- 1/2 C mint (minced)
- 1/4 C Italian parsley (minced)
- 1/2 C panko* *(Japanese bread crumbs)*
- 1/2 C pine nuts* (toasted lightly)
- 4 lamb racks (6 oz each)
- 2 TBSP Dijon mustard
- 1 TBSP garlic (minced)
- 1 TBSP shallots (minced)
- 1/2 C Washington State Cabernet Sauvignon
- 3 TBSP fresh thyme (finely chopped)
- 1/2 C beef stock
- 1/4 C unsalted butter
- olive oil
- salt and pepper

Preheat oven to 375 degrees.

To make crust add the mint, parsley, panko and pine nuts to a food processor and blend until crust is fine. Place mixture on a large plate.

(continued on next page)   *see Appendix

Mint and Nut Crusted Rack of Lamb with Russian Banana Fingerling Potato Purée *continued*

Season lamb racks with salt and pepper. Heat a heavy-bottomed saucepan to medium-high heat. Add 1 tablespoon olive oil. Place lamb racks in pan, fat cap side down first. Sear until racks are thoroughly brown, turn over and place in oven. Turn once during cooking process to ensure even cooking.

Remove from oven when lamb racks have almost reached desired temperature (140 degrees for rare; 160 degrees for medium-well). Brush racks lightly with Dijon mustard, then press into the mint crust mixture. Return to oven for 5 minutes with mint crust side facing up.

Remove racks from pan and set aside to rest. Place the pan back on medium-high heat; remove any burned nuts or fat. Add the garlic and shallots to the pan and sauté. Add the wine and reduce by 3/4. Add the thyme and stock and reduce by 3/4. Reduce heat to medium and add the butter. Incorporate until sauce has thickened. Season to taste with salt and pepper.

To serve, cut each 6-ounce rack in half and lay over the Russian Banana Fingerling Potato Purée *(recipe follows)*. Drizzle sauce around the racks and serve immediately.
(continued below)

Mint and Nut Crusted Rack of Lamb with Russian Banana Fingerling Potato Purée *continued*

Russian Banana Fingerling Potato Purée

3 lbs Russian Banana Fingerling potatoes* (peeled)
2 C butter
2 C cream
salt and pepper

Add potatoes to a saucepot and cover with water. Cook potatoes until fork tender. Strain.

Heat cream and butter. Then mix with potatoes until desired consistency. Season with salt and pepper.

Russian Banana Fingerling potatoes are preferred for this recipe and can be found at specialty grocery stores. (Yukon Gold potatoes may be substituted.) See Appendix.

Serves 4 to 6

SALUTÉ OF BELLEVUE

Saluté of Bellevue
10134 Main Street
Bellevue, WA 98004

425-688-7613

Lunch
Mon-Fri 11:30am-2pm

Dinner
Nightly 5pm-10pm

Raffaele Calise is originally from the island of Ischia off the coast of Naples. He came to Seattle in 1980 after working as a chef in Europe. In 1984 he opened the legendary Saluté Ristorante Italiano near the University Village. Raffaele won several awards for his traditional Italian cooking and was voted one of the 50 best chefs in the United States by GQ magazine. Saluté became a favorite place to eat for the Italian crew who raced the UW for the Windermere Cup in 1987. Raffaele also opened up La Dolce Vita where former UW President Gerberding often came in for lunch. He opened 3 other restaurants in the Seattle area before opening Saluté of Bellevue in 1996. This is a quaint Italian-style villa with great food!

Italian Meatballs

- 1 lb ground beef
- 3 eggs
- 3/4 C Parmesan cheese (grated)
  (or use half Parmesan and half Romano)
- 1 C corn flakes
- 1 C bread (soaked in milk and well-drained)
- 2 TBSP cream
- 1 tsp salt
- 1/2 tsp pepper
- 2 cloves garlic (chopped)
- 3 TBSP parsley
- oil for frying

Place all ingredients in a large bowl. Blend well.

Form into balls, 1-1/2" in diameter.

Brown in deep oil, and drop into spaghetti sauce.

Simmer in sauce for 45 minutes.

Serves 4 to 6

SKYCITY AT THE NEEDLE

SkyCity at the Needle
203 6th Ave N
Seattle, WA 98109-5005

206-905-2100

Hours of operation vary
seasonally

All Major Cards Accepted

www.spaceneedle.com

skyCity™

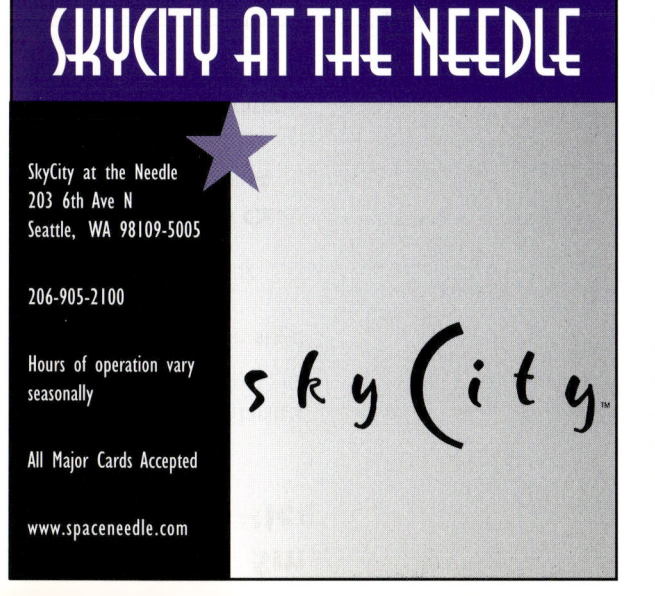

Take in the splendor of the Puget Sound area from SkyCity, the Space Needle's "all-new" revolving restaurant. Located 500 feet above Seattle, SkyCity features many exclusive and signature menu items and celebrates Pacific Northwest cuisine with freshness and dazzling flavor prepared by Chef Gerard Bengle.

The decor is 1960's retro inspired; however, the mood is distinctively modern. Breathtaking views are guaranteed from all tables. Your elevator ride and Observation Deck visit are complimentary when dining at SkyCity. Join us for lunch, dinner, or weekend brunch.

Alderwood Smoked Salmon with Sushi Rice Cakes

2 lbs fresh salmon   sesame oil *(for searing)*

Marinate salmon in Marinade overnight.

Marinade
3/4 C brown sugar	1 TBSP sherry
1/4 C salt	1 TBSP water
2 TBSP honey	2 TBSP garlic (chopped)

Sushi Rice Cakes
2 C Nikko rice*   rice wine vinegar

Prepare Nikko rice according to package instructions EXCEPT replace 1/3 of the water with rice wine vinegar. Press into a 1-inch thick layer. **Refrigerate overnight.** Cut into crescents.

Hot smoke the salmon on your BBQ. While salmon is cooking, sear the rice cakes in sesame oil. Place rice cake on a plate. Top with hot smoked salmon and serve with your favorite vegetable or a light summer salad.

Serves 4   *see Appendix

SOSTANZA

Sostanza Trattoria
Madison Park
1927 43rd East
Seattle, WA 98112

206-324-9701

Dinner
Mon-Sat 5pm-9:30pm

Accepts Major Credit Cards

Sostanza Trattoria is located in one of Seattle's most charming neighborhoods. This two-story Italian Trattoria overlooks Madison Beach and Lake Washington. Sostanza features fireside dining in winter and patio or balcony dining in season. Chef Lorenzo and his staff cater to locals and food aficionados from afar, offering central and northern Italian fare. They offer a full bar, wine cellar and private dining for your special gathering.

Sostanza was honored with a "Top 20 of Seattle" by Gourmet Magazine in 1998.

Stuffed Pork Loin

Four (6 oz) boneless pork loins
4 slices Fontina cheese
4 slices prosciutto
4 fresh sage leaves
2 bunches spinach (cooked, coarsely chopped and strained)
freshly ground black pepper
salt
1 C butter (1/2 C for sautéing and 1/2 C for sauce)
4 shallots (peeled and finely diced)
1 C red wine
1 C veal stock
1/2 C all-purpose flour (for dusting)

Place pork loin between two sheets of plastic wrap and pound until thin.

Place a slice of Fontina and prosciutto on each pork loin. Add sage leaf and cooked spinach. Roll pork loin and tie with kitchen string. Salt and pepper, dust with flour.

Melt 1/2 C butter in a large skillet and cook pork over medium heat turning frequently, until golden brown. Remove from skillet, place in oven-safe dish. Place in 350-degree oven for 10 to 12 minutes. In the same skillet, add shallots, red wine, veal stock, 1/2 C butter and reduce until thick.

Slice pork loin into one-inch medallions. Pour sauce over.
Wine Suggestion: Medium-bodied red such as Vino Nobile di Montepulciano Bindella

Serves 4

WASHINGTON STARS

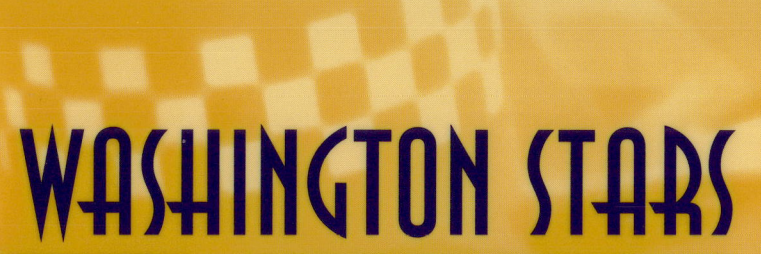

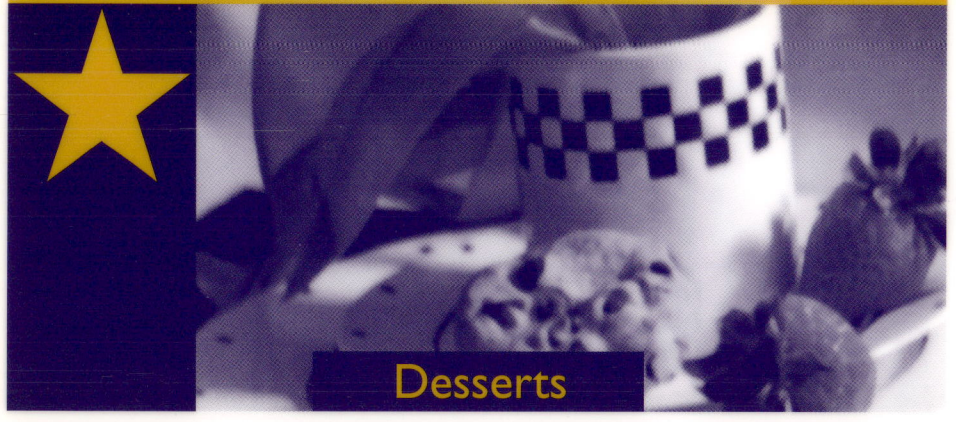

Desserts

THE C SHOP

The C Shop
4825 Alderson Road
Birch Bay, WA 98230
360-371-2070

Open Mid-June to Labor Day

Candy Shop
Open daily 1pm-10pm

Cafe
(Offering baked goods, sandwiches, espresso, floats, and more.)
Thurs, Fri, Sat & Mon
11am-10pm
Sun 1pm-10pm
Pizza Served 5pm-10pm

The C Shop is a family owned business that has been bringing delicious treats to Birch Bay for 30 years. Separated into two sections, the Candy Shop and the Cafe, each serves up home-made quality that is suited to this family resort community. Each recipe is honed to perfection, and every year they come up with new creations.

"What does the name stand for? Well, The C Shop has a number of meanings. Naturally, we are a *Candy* store, and at The C Shop the customer gets to *See* the products being made. Also, we are by the *Sea*; we are a *Corner* store and just think of all the candy that starts with the letter 'C'. Essentially, it stands for anything and everything that you can think of that is part of what makes The C Shop *A Whale of a Place to Go*!"

Carmel Apples

12 to 14 small Granny Smith apples
Popsicle sticks
2 C sugar
3/4 C light corn syrup
1/2 C butter
1 can (8 to 10 oz) evaporated milk
1 C cream

Prepare apples by washing, drying and inserting Popsicle sticks. (Apples need to be dry when dipped.)

In a saucepan, mix sugar, corn syrup, butter and evaporated milk. Bring to a boil over low to medium heat stirring CONSTANTLY. Use a pastry brush dipped in water to wash down the sides of the pan and to also wash the stir spoon (a high-heat spatula or wooden spoon works best) so no sugar crystals remain.

Gradually stir in cream without loosing the boil. Continue to stir as mixture thickens. Cook to 243 degrees *(best measured with a digital candy thermometer for accuracy)*. Turn off heat. Stir a bit more to avoid scorching.

Dip apples in carmel and set on buttered surface to set up. (Any excess carmel may be poured into a buttered pan and cut into carmel pieces when cool.)

Serves 12 to 14

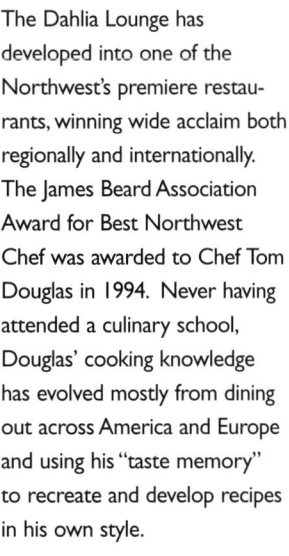

DAHLIA LOUNGE

dahlia lounge
SEATTLE

Dahlia Lounge
2001 4th Avenue
Seattle, WA 98101

206-682-4142

Lunch
Mon-Fri 11:30am-2:30pm

Dinner
Sun-Thurs 5:30pm-10pm
Fri-Sat 5:30pm-11pm

www.tomdouglas.com

The Dahlia Lounge has developed into one of the Northwest's premiere restaurants, winning wide acclaim both regionally and internationally. The James Beard Association Award for Best Northwest Chef was awarded to Chef Tom Douglas in 1994. Never having attended a culinary school, Douglas' cooking knowledge has evolved mostly from dining out across America and Europe and using his "taste memory" to recreate and develop recipes in his own style.

In addition to the Dahlia Lounge Tom owns Etta's Seafood and The Palace Kitchen.

White Chocolate Bread Pudding
(Valentine's Day Recipe)

1 loaf (approximately 3 C) white bread, (cut into small cubes, crusts removed)
6 egg yolks
2 eggs
1/3 C sugar
1 TBSP vanilla extract
2 1/4 C heavy cream
3/4 C milk
7-1/2 oz white chocolate (chopped)

In a metal mixing bowl, with a whisk, combine all ingredients except the bread and chocolate, and place over a pot of simmering (not boiling) water. Heat the custard until warm, whisking occasionally. Add the chocolate and whisk until completely melted.

Fill six buttered *ramekins* (individual dishes used for baking and serving) about halfway with the bread cubes. Pour in some of the custard, pressing down on the bread with a ladle. Wait for the bread to absorb most of the custard, and then pour in the remaining custard, making sure the bread is immersed in the liquid.

Place ramekins on a baking sheet and cover with foil. Bake at 275 degrees for 1 hour, then uncover and bake for an additional 15 minutes. The pudding should be just firm to the touch, and no liquid should appear.

(continued on next page)

DAHLIA LOUNGE

Dahlia Lounge
2001 4th Avenue
Seattle, WA 98101

206-682-4142

Lunch
Mon-Fri 11:30am-2:30pm

Dinner
Sun-Thurs 5:30pm-10pm
Fri-Sat 5:30pm-11pm

www.tomdouglas.com

dahlia lounge

SEATTLE

Tom Douglas has helped to define the Northwest style, or "Pacific Rim Cuisine" as it is sometimes called. Tom's creativity with local ingredients and his respect for Seattle's ethnic traditions have helped put his three restaurants on the national culinary map.

In May of 1999, Tom introduced a specialty food line of rubs for fish, meat and poultry. *Tom Douglas' Rub with Love* spice rubs are available in six different flavors for lamb, pork, steak, chicken, seafood and salmon. Three different kinds of *Tom Douglas Redhook Barbecue Sauces*, made with Redhook's premium beers, were introduced in February of 2001.

Let cool for 15 minutes before serving, or cool completely and keep in the refrigerator for the next day. If serving the next day, **take them out of the refrigerator 2 hours before needed**, then place them in a 300-degree oven for 2 minutes before serving.

Serve with White Chocolate Sauce *(recipe below)*. Fresh or dried berries are a great garnish—and they taste good too!

White Chocolate Sauce
1 C heavy cream
12 oz white chocolate, chopped (can substitute dark chocolate)

Heat the cream until just simmering. Place chocolate in a bowl. Pour cream over the chocolate and stir until completely melted. Keep at room temperature until ready to serve, or cool completely and store in the refrigerator. If serving the next day, warm the sauce by putting it in a metal bowl and place over a pot of simmering (not boiling) water until completely melted, stirring occasionally.

Serves 6

THE FAMOUS NORTHWEST CATERING CO.

The Famous Northwest
Catering Company
3131 E Madison, Suite 101
Arboretum Court
Seattle, WA 98112

206-324-3663

Cafe Hours
Mon-Fri 8am-6pm
Sat 9am-4pm

The
Famous
Northwest™
CATERING COMPANY

The Famous Northwest Catering Company Cafe, located on East Madison in the Arboretum Court, is open Monday through Saturday.

The cafe features fresh soups, sandwiches, salads, desserts and other gourmet food products.

In addition to the cafe, The Famous Northwest Catering Company is a full-service catering company devoted to making your event a wonderful experience.

Vanilla Bean Cheesecake with Fresh Fruit Topping

Line the bottom of a 9" springform pan (2-1/2" deep), with parchment paper. Wrap the outside of the pan in foil to make it water-tight.

Crust
1-1/2 C graham cracker crumbs
1 TBSP sugar
1/4 C unsalted butter, melted

Toss ingredients together and press into the bottom of the pan. Pre-bake the crust at 350 degrees for about 10 minutes, or until lightly browned. Set aside to cool.

Filling
3 lbs cream cheese
1-2/3 C sugar
2 TBSP cornstarch
1/2 C sour cream
5 large eggs
the insides of one whole vanilla bean

Soften the cream cheese, either by leaving out at room temperature or by microwaving it. Process in a mixer or food processor. Mix in the rest of the ingredients being careful not to overwhip. *(continued on next page)*

THE FAMOUS NORTHWEST CATERING CO.

The Famous Northwest
Catering Company
3131 E Madison, Suite 101
Arboretum Court
Seattle, WA 98112

206-324-3663

Cafe Hours
Mon-Fri 8am-6pm
Sat 9am-4pm

The
Famous
Northwest™
CATERING COMPANY

The Famous Northwest Catering Company is a premier Seattle-area caterer with over 20 years experience. They pride themselves on the quality and freshness of their foods.

All of their items are tastefully presented on beautifully garnished trays, platters and baskets.

Each employee at Northwest Catering is dedicated to making your event a success with their outstanding service and delicious food.

Vanilla Bean Cheesecake with Fresh Fruit Topping *continued*

Pour into prepared springform pan. Then, place the springform pan into a larger pan filled halfway with water. Place all this into a 350-degree oven and bake approximately 1-3/4 to 2 hours, or until a knife, inserted in center of cheesecake, comes out clean. Remove the foil.

Chill overnight.

When it's well-chilled, and you are ready to serve, remove the springform from the sides.

Topping
2 pints fresh berries
(frozen fruit may be substituted when fresh berries are not available)

1/2 C sugar
1/8 C Grand Marnier *(if desired)*

Prepare fruit and mix with sugar, "bruising" the fruit slightly. Add Grand Marnier. Cover and let stand for about one hour. If you intend to use the entire cheesecake fairly soon, you can pour entire mixture over the top of the cheesecake. Otherwise, spoon the fruit mixture over the individual pieces just before serving.

Store the unused fruit mixture and cheesecake in the refrigerator.

THE HERBFARM

The Herbfarm
14590 NE 145th St
Woodinville, WA 98072

425-485-5300

Reservations: required
(taken daily 10am-5pm)

Dinner
Thurs-Sun

MC, Visa & AmEx

www.theherbfarm.com

The Herbfarm's Executive Chef Jerry Traunfeld won the James Beard Award for Best American Chef from the Northwest region. He is an expert on culinary herbs and author of the award-winning "The Herbfarm Cookbook."

For sixteen years, The Herbfarm Restaurant has selected the best from farm, forest, and sea to create thematic 9-course dinners showcasing the culinary riches of the Pacific Northwest.

The Herbfarm wraps you in romantic surroundings, an experience featured in every major American food publication. Let The Herbfarm weave you into the fabric of an enchanted evening you'll long remember.

Lemon Verbena-Yogurt Panna Cotta

2 C whole milk
1 pkg unflavored gelatin
1/2 C sugar
Five 4" sprigs fresh lemon verbena
    (or substitute grated zest of 2
    lemons)

2 C plain yogurt
1 pint fresh berries, such as raspberries
    or sliced strawberries

Pour 1/2 cup milk into a small bowl, sprinkle it with the gelatin and set aside for 5 minutes to soften.

Bring the remaining milk to a boil with the sugar in a small saucepan. Stir in lemon verbena sprigs (or zest) and the gelatin. Cover and remove from heat. Let the verbena steep for 15 minutes, then strain the mixture.

Whisk the yogurt in a mixing bowl until smooth. Slowly whisk in the milk mixture.

Pour into 8 lightly oiled 4-ounce ramekins or custard cups. Chill for at least 4 hours. When ready to serve, unmold the Panna Cotta onto serving plates and surround with the fresh berries.

Serves 8

MACRINA BAKERY & CAFE

Macrina Bakery & Café
Belltown Location
2408 1st Ave
Seattle, WA 98121
206-448-4032

Queen Anne Location
615 West McGraw
Seattle, WA 98119
206-283-5900

Hours
Mon-Sat 7am-7pm
Sun 8am-7pm

A graduate of the California Culinary Academy, Leslie Mackie opened Macrina Bakery and Café in 1993. Macrina is best known for its rustic European breads and pastries which are baked fresh daily and can be special-ordered with 48 hours notice.

The Café specializes in hearty soups, Mediterranean salads, quiche, vegetable galettes and many assorted sandwiches made on their own fresh baked bread. The take-out selection has a variety of house-made hors d'oeuvres, spreads, olive oils, local honeys and local jams.

Cherry Almond Scones

These are my friend Andrew's favorite breakfast snacks. They're not overly sweet and have a more biscuit-like texture than most other scones. Enjoy them on their own, or perhaps alongside eggs scrambled with fontina and apple pork sausage.

1/2 C dried, tart and sweet cherries
1/2 C almonds
3 C all-purpose, unbleached flour
1/2 C granulated sugar
2 tsp baking powder
1 tsp baking soda
12 TBSP (1-1/2 sticks) butter, chilled

1 egg
3/4 C buttermilk
1 tsp pure vanilla extract
1/4 tsp pure almond extract
egg wash
    (made with 1 egg and 1 tsp water)
1/4 C coarse raw sugar

Place cherries in a small bowl and cover with warm water. Let soak for 10 minutes. Next, drain the plumped cherries and check for pits. Coarsely chop cherries and set aside.

Preheat oven to 350 degrees. Place almonds on a rimmed baking sheet and toast for approximately 15 minutes, or until golden brown. Let cool, then coarsely chop and set aside.

(continued on next page)

MACRINA BAKERY & CAFE

Macrina Bakery & Café
Belltown Location
2408 1st Ave
Seattle, WA 98121
206-448-4032

Queen Anne Location
615 West McGraw
Seattle, WA 98119
206-283-5900

Hours
Mon-Sat 7am-7pm
Sun 8am-7pm

Ms. Mackie began her culinary career as an apprentice at Ernie's Restaurant in San Francisco and later moved to Boston, where she worked at the Bostonian Hotel and Biba Restaurant. She is an active member of the Bread Bakers Guild and Les Dames d'Escoffier.

Leslie recently had the honor of being included in the "Baking with Julia" television series and companion book.

Cherry Almond Scones *continued*

In a medium bowl, sift flour, granulated sugar, baking powder and baking soda. Toss with your hands to combine.

Slice chilled butter into 1/4-inch pieces and drop into bowl of dry ingredients. Using a pastry cutter or fork, cut butter into mixture until texture is coarse and crumbly. Add the chopped cherries and almonds and mix with a wooden spoon.

In a small bowl; combine egg, buttermilk, vanilla extract and almond extract. Mix with a whisk. Add to dry ingredients and mix gently with a wooden spoon just until dough comes together. Take care not to over mix the dough.

Preheat oven to 375 degrees.

Coat your hands with flour and pull dough from bowl onto a floured surface. Knead the dough for a few minutes, folding and flattening it several times, until dough becomes moldable. Dust the work surface with a little more flour and roll the dough out to 1-inch thickness. Using a round biscuit cutter (about 3 inches across), cut 8 to 10 scones from the dough. Place scones on a lined, rimmed baking sheet. Brush with egg wash and sprinkle coarse raw sugar over the tops. Bake on center rack of oven for 20 to 25 minutes, or until golden brown.

Makes 8 to 10 round scones

THE MALTBY CAFE

Maltby Cafe
8809 Maltby Road
Maltby, WA 98290

425-483-3123

Open Daily 7am-3pm

Breakfast
Mon-Fri 7am-11:20am
Sat-Sun Served all day

Lunch
Every Day 11:30-3pm

The Maltby Cafe

It's hands-on ownership at The Maltby Cafe, with Sandra Albright and Tana Baumler working either in the kitchen or up front. The third owner, Barbara Peter, handles the books. A friendship that started in 1980 as soccer teammates led to the restaurant partnership in 1988. Purchased shortly after being remodeled by the previous owner, a new menu and changes in service led to the popularity the restaurant enjoys today.

Using only the best ingredients, they will satisfy your hunger for home-style cooking. Your visit to The Maltby Cafe will be a one-of-a-kind experience you will want to try again and again.

Maltby Cafe Marionberry Pie

1/2 tsp salt
2 C flour
1/4 C shortening
1/2 C butter
1/4 C water with 1 tsp vinegar

4 C marionberries or blackberries
3/4 C sugar
1 TBSP tapioca
1 TBSP flour

Mix salt and flour in a medium bowl. Cut in shortening and butter. Slowly add water-vinegar mixture and mix with fork until dough forms a ball.

Divide dough and roll out into two rounds. Line an 8-inch pie pan with half of the dough.

Mix berries with the sugar. Add tapioca and flour. Gently mix and pour into lower crust.

Cover with top crust and cut vents in the top. Bake in a preheated 325-degree oven for 45 minutes.

Serves 6 to 8

SALISH LODGE & SPA

Salish Lodge & Spa
6501 Railroad Ave SE
Snoqualmie, WA 98065

1-800-2-SALISH
1-800-272-5474
425-888-2556

MAIN DINING ROOM
Breakfast
Mon-Fri 7am-11am
Sat-Sun 7am-2pm
Dinner
Mon-Sun 5pm-10pm

ATTIC CAFE
11am-1am

www.salishlodge.com

Each of the 91 guest rooms at Salish Lodge & Spa features a bedside wood-burning fireplace, two-person whirlpool tub, goosedown comforter, and a balcony or window seat.

The resort offers a variety of recreational activities, treatments at the award-winning Spa, contemporary Northwest cuisine, and personalized service.

For the eighth annual Gold List, 29,000 subscribers to Condé Nast Traveler participated in its annual Readers' Poll and have chosen the best of the best in travel. Salish Lodge & Spa was named one of the world's best resorts in five categories: rooms, service, restaurants, location and activities in the January 2002 issue of the publication.

Beignets and Chocolate Coffee Ice Cream

Chef Mike Davis has created this dessert, which features culinary icons from his childhood and from his home of 10 years—beignets from Louisiana and coffee from Seattle. "Donuts and coffee" will never be seen in the same light again!

Beignets

- 1-1/2 C warm water
- 1/4 oz active dry yeast
- 1/2 C sugar
- 1/2 tsp salt
- 1 whole egg
- 1 C evaporated milk
- 7 C all-purpose flour
- 1/4 C soft shortening
- oil to fry
- powdered sugar

Place the warm water in a mixing bowl. Spread the yeast evenly over the water and let bloom for 5 minutes.

Add the sugar, salt, egg and milk to the yeast and blend well with a whisk. Add half the flour and beat until smooth. Add the shortening and the remaining flour and beat with a large spoon until flour is thoroughly mixed in.

Cover this mixture with plastic and **chill overnight**.

(continued on next page)

SALISH LODGE & SPA

Salish Lodge & Spa
6501 Railroad Ave SE
Snoqualmie, WA 98065

1-800-2-SALISH
1-800-272-5474
425-888-2556

MAIN DINING ROOM
Breakfast
Mon-Fri 7am-11am
Sat-Sun 7am-2pm
Dinner
Mon-Sun 5pm-10pm

ATTIC CAFE
11am-11pm

www.salishlodge.com

Under the culinary leadership of Chef Mike Davis, the Salish Lodge & Spa now has one of the most creative menus in the Pacific Northwest. To complement the hotel's extensive wine collection, Chef Mike has focused on the marriage of food and wine in each of his signature dishes, which include a duet of foie gras, mint and nut crusted rack of lamb, and smoked salmon chowder.

Born in San Diego and raised in Southern Washington, Chef Mike spent his formative years (ages 9 to 18) in Louisiana and started cooking in traditional Cajun kitchens at the age of 13.

Under Chef Mike's tenure, The Dining Room has received acclaim from *Seattle Magazine*, *Seattle Weekly*, *Eastside Journal*, *Seattle PI*, *Northwest Palate*, and *Northwest Travel*.

Beignets and Chocolate Coffee Ice Cream *cont.*

To make beignets, roll out the dough on a floured work surface to 1/8-inch thick and cut into 2-inch squares.

To cook, heat up fryer oil or shortening to 375 degrees. Gently place squares in oil. Cook until each side is golden brown. Beignets should puff up like "pillows."

Remove from oil and place onto a paper towel to drain excess oil.

To serve, dust beignets heavily with powdered sugar.

Chocolate Coffee Ice Cream
8 oz semi-sweet chocolate
4 C milk
1/2 C instant espresso
2 vanilla beans, split lengthwise
4 C heavy cream

6 egg yolks
1-1/4 C sugar
1 C whipped cream
1/4 C powdered sugar

(continued on next page)

SALISH LODGE & SPA

Salish Lodge & Spa
6501 Railroad Ave SE
Snoqualmie, WA 98065

1-800-2-SALISH
1-800-272-5474
425-888-2556

MAIN DINING ROOM
Breakfast
Mon-Fri 7am-11am
Sat-Sun 7am-2pm
Dinner
Mon-Sun 5pm-10pm

ATTIC CAFE
11am-11pm

www.salishlodge.com

Consistently ranked among the best small resorts in the world, Salish Lodge & Spa is located 30 miles east of Seattle, overlooking the 268-foot Snoqualmie Falls (one hundred feet higher than the famed Niagara Falls).

Snoqualmie Falls, one of Washington state's most popular scenic attractions, lures 1.5 million visitors every year.

In the 1890s, Charles H. Baker first saw the falls and a dream took shape. In 1898, construction began on the power plant in an effort to harness the power of the flowing water. It became an engineering marvel as the construction required excavation through solid rock.

Beignets and Chocolate Coffee Ice Cream *cont.*

Melt the chocolate using a double-boiler method; set aside.

In a heavy bottom saucepot; add the milk, espresso, vanilla beans and heavy cream. Bring to a boil.

In a mixing bowl, combine the egg yolks and sugar. Whip until smooth. Temper the egg mixture with the cream. Place this mixture back onto the stove. Heat until mixture is thick enough to coat the back of a spoon without running. DO NOT BOIL. Remove from heat, whisk in the chocolate then transfer to an ice bath to chill.

Once chilled, place ingredients into an ice cream maker to finish, following manufacturer's directions. Store in freezer.

For garnish, whip remaining cup of cream and powdered sugar in a mixing bowl until firm. Place ice cream in individual cups and dollop with whipped cream. Serve with warm beignets.

Serves 6 to 8

SAVORY FAIRE

Savory Faire
135 S Main Street
Montesano, WA 98563

360-249-3701

<u>Hours</u>
Open Monday-Friday
10:30am-3:30pm

Visa, MC, AmEx, Discover

www.savoryfaire.com

Savory Faire has been in business for 18 years producing handcrafted quality breads, soups, salads and desserts. The restaurant is a family affair with Candi (owner and pastry chef); husband and high school teacher, Randy (maker of the delicious breads every morning before school); son, Josh (master of the mirage of soups); and daughter Heather, (buyer and merchandiser of the gift shop).

Savory Faire has had a recipe published in *Bon Appetit*, been in *Northwest Best Places* for 12 years and has been featured in several travel magazines. They recently published their first *Savory Faire Cookbook*.

Heather and her husband are both UW graduates.

Amaretto Bread Pudding

1 loaf of white bread *(with crust)* (cubed)
1 quart Half and Half
1-1/2 C sugar
4 eggs
2 TBSP almond extract
1 C almonds (sliced)
whipping cream for serving *(optional)*

Place bread cubes, Half and Half, sugar, eggs, almond extract and almonds in a large mixing bowl. Mix until well combined. Pour mixture into a buttered 9"x13" pan. Bake at 350 degrees for 35 minutes or until set.

When pudding is almost finished baking, prepare the sauce below.

> **Sauce**
> 1 C butter
> 2 C powdered sugar
> 1 egg
> 1/3 C Amaretto liqueur
>
> Place butter in a saucepan and melt slowly. Add powdered sugar and beaten egg. Mix quickly so that the egg doesn't cook before it's incorporated. Cook until smooth and incorporated. Add the liqueur.

Cut pudding into 12 squares and serve warm with warmed sauce and whipping cream.

Serves 12

SUNFLOUR BAKERY & CAFE

Sunflour Bakery & Cafe
3118 NE 65th St
Seattle, WA 98115

206-525-1034

Dining Room
Breakfast Tues-Fri: 8am-11:30am
Brunch Sat & Sun: 8am-3pm
Lunch Tues-Fri: 11:30am-3pm
Dinner Tues-Sat: 5pm-9pm

Bakery & Espresso
Tues-Sat: 7am-9pm
Sun: 8am-3pm

Closed Mondays

Sunflour

Bakery & Cafe

The Sunflour Bakery & Cafe is a casual, well-priced neighborhood restaurant that serves great food with outstanding service in a cozy comfortable environment.

The dining room has the feel of a European bistro with a warm fire blazing on chilly nights and the smell of bread baking.

The Sunflour Bakery & Cafe is owned by Blake and Mary Morrison. Mary graduated from the U of W in 1990. Blake's dad, Ken Morrison is a retired Associate Dean of the U of W Dental School.

Grand Marnier-Chocolate Cheesecake

Crust
1 C chocolate cookie crumbs   4 TBSP unsalted butter, firm

In a food processor with chopping blades, combine cookie crumbs and butter. Process 5 to 10 seconds. Press into the bottom of a parchment-lined 10" springform pan. Bake at 350 degrees for 10 minutes. Set aside to cool.

Ganache
9 oz semi-sweet chocolate   2 oz unsalted butter
10 oz heavy cream

Place cream in a small saucepan over medium heat. Chop chocolate into medium-sized pieces and place in food processor with chopping blades. Process until reduced to a coarse meal. Do not over work. Place butter in a medium bowl.

When cream reaches simmer, remove from heat and pour directly into running processor with chocolate and allow to run for 15 seconds. Pour directly over butter and allow butter to melt. Stir occasionally. Allow to cool slightly.

(continued on next page)

SUNFLOUR BAKERY & CAFE

Sunflour Bakery & Cafe
3118 NE 65th St
Seattle, WA 98115

206-525-1034

DINING ROOM
Breakfast Tues-Fri 8am-11:30am
Brunch Sat & Sun 8am-3pm
Lunch Tues-Fri 11:30am-3pm
Dinner Tues-Sat: 5pm-9pm

BAKERY & ESPRESSO
Tues-Sat 7am-9pm
Sun 8am-3pm

Closed Mondays

The culinary emphasis at The Sunflour is to provide simple food, properly prepared and made with the best available ingredients. The dinner menu offers specialty items like Dungeness crabcakes, braised lamb shanks and mushroom sage risotto. There are always several vegetarian choices on the menu, and a well-rounded wine list that offers exceptional value.

Children are welcome and are offered their own menu.

All the breads, pastries, desserts and pies served in the restaurant are made in their in-house bakery.

Grand Marnier-Chocolate Cheesecake *cont.*

When slightly cool, pour about 1/4-inch deep over crust in spring form pan. Place in refrigerator and allow to firm up.

Cake

- 16 oz cream cheese
- 1 C sugar
- 6 egg yolks
- zest of one orange
- 2 TBSP Grand Marnier
- 1-1/2 tsp vanilla
- 1/4 tsp salt
- 3 C sour cream

Place the cream cheese, sugar and egg yolks in processor and blend until free of lumps. Zest orange directly into processor bowl. Add Grand Marnier, vanilla, salt and sour cream and blend until smooth. Pour into spring form pan.

Wrap the outside of a spring form pan in two layers of foil. Make sure the foil reaches the rim. Place this pan in a larger pan of very hot water. Water should reach 2/3 up the side of the pan. Place this in a 350-degree oven and bake for 50 minutes. Turn oven off and allow it to sit for an additional 30 to 60 minutes in the oven. Refrigerate.

To serve, cut with a hot, wet knife.

WASHINGTON STARS

Appendix

Where to Find Special Ingredients

Ingredient	Larry's Markets	QFC	Top Foods	Uwajimaya	Whole Foods
Achiote spice bar (annatto seed paste)	x				
Ahi tuna	x	x	x		x
American Caviars (seasonal)	x	x	SO		x
Calamari	x	x	x		x
Chervil (herb)	x	SO	x		x

SO = special order

Where to Find Special Ingredients *cont.*

Ingredient	Larry's Markets	QFC	Top Foods	Uwajimaya	Whole Foods
DaVinci Apple Syrup (www.davincigourmet.com)					x
Duck fat	SO				x
Frisée	x				x
Gruyere Cheese	x	x	x		x
Gyoza skins	x	x	x	x	x
Lemon Grass	x	x	x	x	x
Mortadella (smoked Italian sausage)	x	SO	x		x
Mussels	x	x	x	x	x
Nikko rice	x	x	x	x	x
Nori sheet (dried seaweed)	x	x	x	x	x

Where to Find Special Ingredients *cont.*

Ingredient	Larry's Markets	QFC	Top Foods	Uwajimaya	Whole Foods
Old Bay Seasonings	x	x	x		x
Panko (Japanese bread crumbs)	x	x	x		
Pickled red ginger	x	x		x	x
Pine Nuts	x	x	x	x	x
Russian Banana Fingerling Potatoes	SO	SO			x
Thai fish sauce (red curry sauce)	x		x	x	x
Truffle butter					x
Veal stock	x	x		x	x
Veal top round roast	x	SO			x
White truffle oil	x				x

SO = special order

Specialty Food Stores

The following list of stores is by no means complete.
It is intended as a basic reference for your convenience.

★

For a complete and up-to-date listing, check out the websites listed below.

Haggen Food & Pharmacy (www.haggen.com)
(See Top Food & Drug for items carried as they are the same company with store locations in northern Washington and Portland, OR)

Larry's Market (www.larrysmarkets.com)   Store
   Bellevue (699 120th Ave NE) 425-453-0600
   Kirkland *(Totem Lake)* (12320 120th Place NE) 425-820-2300
   Queen Anne Marketplace (100 Mercer St. N) 206-213-0778
   Redmond Town Center (7320 170th Ave NE). 425-869-2362
   Seattle *(Oak Tree Plaza)* (10008 Aurora Ave N.). 206-527-5333
   Tukwilla (3725 S. 144th St). 206-242-5290

Specialty Food Stores *continued*

Top Food & Drugs (www.top-foods.com)
    Aberdeen (1213 E. Wishkah St.) 360-532-1830
    Bellevue (15751 NE 15th St). 425-748-1300
    Federal Way (31515 20th Ave. S.) 253-839-9299
    Snohomish (1301 Avenue D). 360-568-1395
    Tacoma (3130 S. 23rd St) 253-591-0155
    Woodinville (17641 Garden Way NE) 425-398-6700

QFC (www.qfconline.com or www.kroger.com)
    Bellevue - Bellevue Village (10116 NE 8th). 425-455-0870
    Kirkland (211 Park Place Center). 425-827-2205
    Redmond (Old) (15800 Redmond Way NE) 425-885-2311
    Redmond (Bella Botega) (8867 161st Ave NE). 425-869-8006
    U Village (2746 NE 45th). 206-523-5160
    Woodinville (14160 NE Woodinville-Duvall Road) 425-485-0119

Specialty Food Stores *continued*

Whole Foods (www.wholefoods.com)
    Seattle *(Roosevelt Square)* (1026 NE 64th Street) 206-985-1500

Uwajimaya, Inc (www.uwajimaya.com)
    Bellevue (15555 NE 24th) *(Corner of 24th & Bel-Red Rd)*. . . . 425-747-9012
    Seattle - *(Downtown)* (600 5th Avenue S, Suite 100) 206-624-6248

Information was accurate at the time of printing, but it is always advisable to call ahead
to see if your ingredient is still stocked by the store listed
or if it needs to be ordered in advance.

★

The University of Washington Alumnae Board is
part of the University of Washington Alumni Association.
This volunteer organization is made up of 35 to 40 women
who each serve a four-year term
with the focus of their time on fundraising.

★

We are one of the top sources of scholarship dollars
available at the University of Washington.
We award the ONLY full-tuition scholarships
from the Alumni Association.

Alumnae Board **UW**

*Please call us or visit our website if you would like more information about
our scholarships, our annual Holiday Fair or would like to volunteer.*

206-543-0540   ★   **www.washington.edu/alumni/alumnae**

Changing Lives—One Scholarship at a Time!

Credits

Julie Myers and Robin Blackbourn
Washington Stars Cookbook Co-Chairs

Julie Myers
Editor

Sandy Teich
"Fine Assistant" to the Editor

Robin Blackbourn
Graphic Design

Sandy Teich ★ Jen Thomas
Jan Rood ★ Jennifer Budnick
Bernadette Anne ★ Gail Pratt
Production Assistants

Special Thanks

Russell Lowell and Ken McNamee
For their additional help and expertise
in this creative endeavor.

★

UW Alumnae Board
For recommending their favorite restaurants.
We hope you enjoy their recipes!

★

Our Families
For their support throughout the
phone-calling, typesetting, cooking, editing, photographing and
proofing, proofing, and more prooofing…!

Our sincerest thanks to everyone
who purchased this cookbook.

★

Without you, our efforts
would be meaningless.

★

Whether you bought this book
as a gift for yourself or someone else,
you have given an additional gift of education
to a deserving UW student.

★

We all thank you for your support.

© 2002 UW Alumni Association (Alumnae Board)

ISBN 0-9704941-1-4

WASHINGTON STARS

Cookbook

Volume 1

ISBN 0-9704941-1-4